FAITH OVER FEAR

A HEALING JOURNEY

By Kimberly DeAnn Bradley Allen

Faith Over Fear: A Healing Journey

DEDICATION

In loving memory of my mom and my dad.

To my mom, Patricia Ann Bradley,
who planted faith in me and taught me to walk with God.
She also gave me strength and resilience that carry me still.
Being born on my mother's 20th birthday ensured that we
had a forever bond; forever connected September 16.

To my dad, Thomas Arthur English, Sr.,
who taught me to completely trust God and to know with
certainty that all things will work together for my good
because of my love for Him.

To Auburn, my soul dog,
my beloved Yorkie who walked beside me for ten beautiful
years before crossing the rainbow bridge. You were my
comfort in silent moments, my companion through joy
and pain, and the little heartbeat at my feet during some
of my hardest days. Your love was a gift, and your memory
remains a warm place in my heart.

To my husband, Danny,
who has stood beside me in love through every season.

And to my children, Zachary and Madison,
my greatest blessings and the reason I fight with courage
every day.
This book is for you. ♥

CONTENTS

Part I - The Diagnosis and Early Journey

Part II - The Healing & Revelation

Closing Sections

"And we know that all things work together for good to them that love God, to them who are the called according to his purpose." – Romans 8:28

IN HONOR OF TWENTY-TWO

"Precious in the sight of the Lord is the death of his saints." – Psalm 116:15

There are twenty-two chapters in this book for a reason. The number 22 carries deep meaning for me. In 2022, I lost both of my parents only ninety-three days apart — my mother on August 22, 2022, and my father on November 23, 2022.

I sat beside them for their final days as they took their last breaths.

That season reshaped my faith and my understanding of eternity. It taught me that God's presence does not leave in loss — it deepens. When I began this book, I knew it would end at twenty-two chapters, because 2022 marked the year God used both grief and grace to prepare me for the healing journey that followed.

Each chapter became part of that story — not just of surviving breast cancer, but of continuing my parents' legacy of faith, peace, and trust in God. Ending at twenty-two is my way of honoring them and the divine symmetry of the life God has written for me.

Author's Note

When I began writing, I wasn't setting out to write a book. I was writing to survive. I was writing to breathe again — to steady my heart when the weight of uncertainty felt too heavy to carry. Each word began as a whispered prayer between me and God, not meant for an audience, but meant to help me remember who He is when fear tried to make me forget.

Some of what you'll read started as journal entries written in the early morning hours, late at night, after doctor's appointments and sleepless prayers. Some were written on days when I felt brave, and others when I felt broken. I didn't know at the time that those raw moments — the quiet tears, the whispered scriptures, the still small voice of peace — were all being woven together into something that would one day become a testimony.

Over time, I began to see a pattern that only God could have designed. Every fear was met with His faithfulness. Every waiting season became a classroom for trust. Every loss prepared my heart for a deeper kind of healing. I learned that faith isn't the absence of fear — it's the decision to trust God right in the middle of it.

This book, *Faith Over Fear*, was born out of that truth. It's more than a timeline of events; it's a mosaic of grace. It's proof that God is present in both the chaos and the calm, in the scans and the silence, in the hospital hallways and in the holy moments of peace that only He can give.

As you read these pages, my hope is that you'll feel God's nearness in your own story. You may not be walking through breast cancer, but we all face moments that test our faith — moments when the future looks uncertain and fear tries to take the lead. My prayer is that as you journey through this devotional, you'll find comfort, courage, and a renewed awareness that you are never walking alone.

Every chapter of this book was written through tears and thanksgiving. Some days I asked God to take the fear away; other days, I thanked Him for the strength to face it. In time, I realized that even unanswered prayers were answered in unexpected ways. God doesn't always remove the storm — sometimes He calms His child instead.

If you are holding this book today, I believe it's not by accident. Maybe you need a reminder that hope still lives here. Maybe you're searching for peace that surpasses understanding, or maybe you simply need to know that even when life changes, God never does. Whatever brought you here, may these words meet you right where you are.

With love, faith, and gratitude for the journey,
Kim

Introduction

T his is not the story I ever imagined I would write. The day I heard the words *"You have breast cancer,"* it felt like the ground shifted beneath me. Life suddenly divided itself into two chapters — **before** and **after** — and I found myself standing in the middle of a moment I never prepared for.

Fear tried to rise.

Questions flooded my mind.

Everything familiar felt fragile.

And yet — in the deepest places of my heart — **God was there.**

He was in the doctor's office.

He was in the waiting rooms.

He was in the sleepless nights.

He was in the moments when I whispered, *"Lord, I don't know what to do."*

He was in the tears I cried softly so no one else would hear.

He was in the quiet strength that held me up when I should have fallen apart.

His presence didn't remove the valley—but it lit the valley.

It steadied me.

It carried me.

It transformed me.

This book is my journal — not polished, not perfect, but **real**.

It holds the raw reflections of a woman walking through diagnosis, treatment, and healing while clinging fiercely to her faith. There were days I felt brave and days I felt broken. Days I could lift my hands in worship, and days when the only prayer I could whisper was, *"Jesus, help me."*

But across every chapter, one truth emerged over and over again:

Weakness is not failure — it is where God's strength becomes undeniable.

I write these pages not just to share my own journey, but to reach for your hand as you walk through yours. Whether you are facing cancer or another kind of valley, my prayer is that you will find hope in these words. I pray you will discover the same truth God revealed to me:

He is faithful — even when fear shouts loudest.

He is near — even when the night feels long.

He is steady — even when the world is shaking.

His promises are true — and His healing is real.

This devotional is a testimony of **faith over fear**, **light in the middle of darkness**, and **grace that meets you in the valley**.

As you read, may you sense God's whisper reminding you:

"Be still and know that I am God." – Psalm 46:10

No matter where you stand right now — at the beginning of your battle, in the middle of it, or on the other side — I pray these pages draw you closer to the One who carried me, comforted me, protected me, healed me, and strengthened me.

You are not alone.

You are not forgotten.

And you are deeply loved by a faithful God.

With love, gratitude, and unwavering faith,

Kim

IT IS WELL: A TESTAMENT OF MIRACLES

Before you begin reading the chapters of this book — before you walk with me into the appointments, the stillness, the fear, the faith, and the healing — I want to testify of God's goodness. Not at the end of my journey, but woven all throughout it.

These are the miracles God performed — the ones the doctors cautioned me about, the ones they prepared me to expect, and the ones God overturned with His own hands.

Every time the medical team spoke a possibility, something in my spirit rose with the same response:

"It is well."

Not because the news was easy.

Not because I understood everything.

Not because I felt brave.

But because I trusted the God who had walked into every room before me.

Here are three miracles that shaped this journey:

1. "We may have to remove the nipple."

I said, "It is well."

God said, "I will preserve you."**

Before surgery, the doctor prepared me for the possibility of losing the nipple.

I took a breath, steadied my heart, and whispered, **"It is well."**

When I woke up, the surgeon walked in smiling: **"We didn't have to take it."**

God preserved what man expected to remove.

2. "You may lose sensation."
I said, "It is well."
God said, "You will feel fully again."**
Before the second surgery, I was told:
"You will likely lose sensation. It happens often."
Once again, my spirit rose in quiet faith:
"It is well."
When I woke up, the news brought tears to my eyes:
"You still have full sensation."
God restored what man predicted I would lose.

3. "You'll need 20 radiation treatments."
I said, "It is well."
God said, "You only need five."**
Twenty treatments.
Twenty days.
Twenty chances for fear to creep in.
But even then, I said:
"It is well."
During my simulation, the doctor reviewed the data again and said, "You don't need twenty. You only need **five**."
God shortened the valley.
God accelerated the healing.
God reduced the burden.
On September 8, I completed my fifth treatment.
And then it was time to ring the bell.

The Three Rings of the Bell
As the nurse guided me to the bell, she explained the meaning behind each ring — something I will never forget.
The First Ring — Victory
A declaration that the battle you endured has come to an end.
A proclamation that you overcame the valley that tried to break you.

The Second Ring — Strength
A recognition of every sleepless night, every tear, every scripture whispered, every fear surrendered, every prayer prayed.

The Third Ring — Hope
A release into your future — and a testimony for every woman who will come behind you.
A reminder that God still heals, God still delivers, and God still comes through.

When I grabbed the rope and rang the bell three times, heaven rang with me.
It wasn't just a ritual.
It wasn't just an ending.
It was God's exclamation mark on my story.
What was meant to break me became the place where God showed Himself mighty.
What was meant to steal my joy became the place where my faith grew roots.
What was meant for evil, God turned for good — again and again.
Before you turn the page and walk into Chapter 1 with me, know this:
This is not a story about cancer.
This is a story about Christ —
a story of faith over fear,
peace over panic,
victory over diagnosis,
and a God who keeps His promises.

Part I - The Diagnosis and Early Journey

 Chapter 1 — Diagnosis Day

Opening Verse

"Be still and know that I am God."
– Psalm 46:10

Journal Entry

On January 16, 2025, I walked into my appointment expecting nothing more than another routine mammogram. I had done this fourteen times before without news, without fear, without even thinking twice. But the fifteenth one changed my life.

What made this moment even more powerful is that I almost didn't go.

For the first time in years, I had considered skipping it. Life felt too busy. I was tired of the routines, the appointments, the constant pressure of balancing work, home, marriage, bills, and my own self-care. Somewhere deep inside I felt a nudge, the still small voice of God whispering, *"Go."* I didn't know it at the time, but that whisper was the first step in saving my life.

When the screening came back abnormal, something inside me shifted. It wasn't fear yet—not in the beginning. It was more like confusion, disbelief, and the quiet understanding that something was happening that I could not control.

Over the next several months, I found myself caught in what felt like an endless loop of tests, scans, biopsies, waiting rooms, and unanswered questions. Each time a result came back "benign but suspicious," I wanted to breathe relief—but I couldn't. It felt as if God was saying, *"Keep going. Keep looking. Keep trusting."*

Even during those uncertain months, God was already orchestrating what I would later recognize as a divine setup.

Then came July 3, 2025. The day the words "you have breast cancer" entered the room and landed in my ears like weights. The world around me suddenly felt heavy, too bright, too quiet all at the same time. But in the middle of that moment—one that should have shaken me—I felt God's presence settle over me like warm oil.

What should have been chaos became stillness.

Danny was sitting next to me when the doctor spoke the words no one ever wants to hear. He grabbed my hand immediately. It was a silent vow—we were about to walk this together. From that moment on, it was me, Danny, and God standing in that exam room.

We didn't call anyone.

We didn't tell our families.

We didn't invite opinions.

We carried this quietly—just the three of us—until we had the strength to share.

Danny never missed a single appointment. Not one. He prayed over me every morning, every meal, and every night. Watching my husband's faith deepen in the middle of my diagnosis was one of the greatest miracles of this journey. Not only was God healing my body—He was strengthening my marriage and the spiritual foundation of our home.

My mother, who was a nurse, would have been right there at my side if she were still alive. I could almost imagine her handing me tissue, coaching me through every medical term, steadying my heart with her calm presence. Losing her in 2022 was one of the greatest heartbreaks of my life—but God showed me that her love hadn't left me.

There was a photo I had looked at dozens of times before, but never noticed the detail until after my diagnosis. In the picture, my mother is leaning her head on my right side—the same side where the cancer was later found. It felt like a holy photograph, a reminder that she was covering me long before I knew I needed it.

And then came the butterfly.

On the day of my first biopsy, as I was walking the dogs, a monarch butterfly landed in the grass and stayed still—almost waiting for me. When I called Danny over and asked if he could see it, he said he didn't see anything at all. I knew then it was meant for me alone. It was as if God and my mother were both whispering,

"You're not alone. I'm right here."

I stood there in awe, tears in my eyes, overwhelmed at the intimacy of God's comfort. He didn't send a storm or a sign written in the clouds—He sent a butterfly. Gentle. Quiet. Personal.

That's how good God is.

He doesn't just show up.

He shows up for *you*.

(Additional Spiritual Reflection)

Looking back, I realized that cancer did not catch God by surprise. He had prepared every step long before I received the diagnosis. From the whisper that pushed me to go to the mammogram, to the sequence of tests that refused to let the cancer remain hidden, to the people He placed in my life for prayer and support—God was already there.

Fear wanted to write my story, but God had already written a better one.

One of the greatest truths I learned in this season is this:

God does not remove every storm—sometimes He calms *you* in the storm.

I found comfort in Scriptures I had read a thousand times but never truly felt until then. Each verse became oxygen to me. Each promise became a rock under my feet. God was not distant. He was near in a way I had never experienced before.

And even though I didn't know what the next steps would be, I knew this:

God does not whisper "go" unless He has already gone before you.

Scripture Meditations

- **Isaiah 41:10** – "Fear thou not; for I am with thee…"
- **Romans 8:28** – "All things work together for good…"
- **Psalm 27:1** – "The Lord is the strength of my life…"
- **Psalm 34:4** – "I sought the Lord, and he heard me…"

Reflecting on these verses anchored my soul. They were not just words—they became weapons.

Reflection Questions

1. What moments in your life felt like interruptions but were really divine interventions?
2. Where is God asking you to trust Him even when you don't understand?
3. How has God shown you His presence in gentle, unexpected ways?
4. What "butterfly moments" has God used to remind you that you're not alone?

Closing Prayer

Father, thank You for meeting me in the places where fear tries to rise. Thank You for Your gentle reminders—through whispers, butterflies, people, and peace—that You never leave me alone. Help me to trust You not only with the diagnosis, but with every detail of my life. Strengthen my heart, calm my mind, and let my faith be louder than my fear. In Jesus' name, amen.

 Chapter 2 — Survival Guide

Opening Verse

"The Lord is my strength and my shield; my heart trusted in him, and I am helped: therefore my heart greatly rejoiceth; and with my song will I praise him."
– Psalm 28:7

Journal Entry

In the days following my diagnosis, everything around me moved in slow motion. People were going about their regular lives — grocery shopping, laughing, driving, planning their weekends — while my world had suddenly shifted into something unfamiliar and fragile. The air felt different. Ordinary moments felt heavier. Even simple tasks like making coffee or folding clothes carried a quiet awareness of the unknown.

I realized quickly that if I was going to endure this season, I needed more than medical appointments and information — I needed a **spiritual survival guide**. Not something written in a book, but something written in my heart.

My survival guide became a lifeline:

Prayer. Scripture. Worship. Boundaries. Stillness. Peace.

It wasn't something I crafted in a single moment. It formed day by day, as God revealed what my soul needed to stay anchored. I learned that in the middle of fear, you must build a place for God to speak. And for me, that place was carved out of intentional choices.

I started praying differently — not long, complicated prayers, but honest ones:

"Lord, I need You."

"Strengthen me."

"Speak to me."

Sometimes my prayers were nothing more than tears. And I learned that God translates tears better than any language.

I also became mindful of what I allowed into my spirit. Music, conversations, social media, news — everything had to pass through a filter of peace. If it fed my fear, I shut it out. If it fed my faith, I welcomed it.

Danny became my prayer partner. We prayed over meals, over my body, over our home, over the journey ahead. His prayers were sometimes quiet, sometimes strong, but always sincere. I watched God strengthen him just as God strengthened me. Fear tried to divide us, but prayer united us.

Worship became another anchor. Not the kind of worship that required a church service or a full band — but quiet worship in the middle of my living room, in my car, or during late nights when sleep felt far away. Songs that reminded me of God's character filled the spaces where anxiety tried to sneak in.

I also had to set new boundaries — emotional, mental, and spiritual. I learned that not everyone has the capacity to walk with you through a valley. Some people carry fear instead of faith. Some mean well but offer stories that plant worry, not hope. God taught me early on to guard my circle.

And then there was stillness.

Stillness became sacred.

Stillness became survival.

Stillness became the place where God reminded me:

"I am here."

This survival guide didn't remove the storm, but it equipped me to stand in it.

One of the most surprising parts of this season was how God worked in quiet, ordinary moments. I remember one morning after my diagnosis, I woke up before the sun and sat on the edge of my bed. The house was silent. My thoughts were loud. I didn't have the words to pray, and I didn't have the strength to pretend I was okay.

As I sat there, a verse rose in my heart:

"Be still, and know that I am God."

It wasn't shouted.

It wasn't dramatic.

It was gentle — a reminder that I didn't have to carry the weight of this alone.

In that stillness, God taught me something important:

Your spirit needs refuge, not noise.

Your faith needs strengthening, not overstimulation.

Your mind needs peace, not panic.

I built habits that protected the fragile parts of my heart:

- I limited conversations that drained my spirit.
- I surrounded myself with believers who spoke life.
- I wrote scriptures on sticky notes and placed them around the house.
- I started journaling my prayers and fears.
- I took deep breaths and reminded myself that God was in the room with me.

Slowly — very slowly — the fear began to loosen its grip. Not because the circumstances changed, but because *I* changed. My survival guide wasn't just something I used; it became who I was becoming through Christ.

Scripture Meditations

- **Philippians 4:13** — "I can do all things through Christ which strengtheneth me."

- **Psalm 91:2** — "I will say of the Lord, He is my refuge and my fortress: my God; in him will I trust."
- **Isaiah 26:3** — "Thou wilt keep him in perfect peace, whose mind is stayed on thee…"
- **Psalm 34:4** — "I sought the Lord, and he heard me, and delivered me from all my fears."

Reflection Questions

1. What would your personal survival guide look like in a season of fear or uncertainty?
2. Which voices in your life strengthen your faith, and which ones weaken it?
3. What habits or boundaries might God be inviting you to set in place?
4. How can you create space for stillness so God can speak to your heart?

Closing Prayer

Lord, thank You for being my refuge and my strength. In moments when fear rises, teach me to anchor myself in Your Word, Your presence, and Your peace. Help me build habits that draw me closer to You and guard my heart from anything that steals my focus. Thank You for being the God who strengthens, sustains, and shields me. Hold me close as I walk through this season with You. In Jesus' name, amen.

CHAPTER 3 — TRUSTING GOD'S WHISPER

Opening Verse

"And after the earthquake a fire; but the Lord was not in the fire: and after the fire a still small voice."
– 1 Kings 19:12

Journal Entry

In the middle of all the noise — the appointments, the waiting, the questions — I learned to quiet myself and listen for God's whisper. It wasn't dramatic. It wasn't loud. It wasn't a sign written across the sky. It was subtle, gentle, and unmistakably divine.

When I think back to January 2025, the beginning of this journey, I remember how close I came to skipping my mammogram. I was tired, distracted, and overwhelmed with life. Nothing inside me felt urgent about the appointment. But in the stillness, I heard a prompting I couldn't shake: *"Go."* Just one simple word... but that whisper saved my life.

I didn't understand the weight of that obedience in the moment. It felt like a routine reminder — the kind you easily ignore. But now, looking back, I see how God used that whisper as the first thread in a tapestry I didn't even know He was weaving.

There were many days when fear shouted louder than peace. Days when the unknown felt bigger than the promises I clung to. But every time anxiety tried to take over, God would gently nudge my heart —

never through force, but through quiet assurance. Sometimes it came through a verse. Sometimes through a song. Sometimes through Danny's voice. But always, it was the same Whisperer.

I learned that God doesn't always guide us with big moments. Sometimes He guides us with the smallest impressions — the ones you could easily miss if you're not listening.

There is something sacred about listening for God in seasons of uncertainty. When life shakes you, His whisper becomes your anchor. It becomes the voice that stands up to fear and says, *"Peace. Be still."*

God reminded me that His whisper has power — not because of its volume, but because of who is speaking.

Trusting His whisper required surrender. It required quieting the noise, tuning out fear, and letting the Holy Spirit lead my steps. And when I obeyed that whisper — without understanding why — I walked right into God's protection, timing, and purpose.

Every step of this journey was marked by His voice — subtle, soft, but steady. It didn't remove the valley, but it carried me through it.

And I learned something priceless:

When you choose to trust God's whisper, you will always find yourself standing exactly where you need to be.

Scripture Meditations

- **Isaiah 30:21** — "This is the way, walk ye in it…"
- **John 10:27** — "My sheep hear my voice…"
- **Psalm 32:8** — "I will instruct thee and teach thee in the way which thou shalt go…"
- **Psalm 46:10** — "Be still, and know that I am God."

Reflection Questions

1. When has God whispered something to your heart that didn't make sense until later?

2. What noise or distractions might you need to silence in order to hear God more clearly?
3. How does God often speak to you — through scripture, people, songs, impressions, or peace?
4. What small act of obedience is God prompting you to take today?

Closing Prayer

Lord, thank You for the gentle ways You speak to my heart. Teach me to slow down, to listen, and to trust Your whisper more than the noise around me. Quiet every fear, every doubt, and every distraction so I can hear You clearly. Give me courage to obey even when I don't understand, knowing Your voice always leads me into purpose and protection. In Jesus' name, amen.

CHAPTER 4 — DIVINE SETUP

(A Walk of Faith – September 3 to July 3)

Opening Verse

*"For I know the thoughts that I think toward you, saith
the Lord, thoughts of peace, and not of evil, to give you
an expected end."*
– Jeremiah 29:11

Journal Entry

The day after Labor Day — September 3, 2024 — is a date I will never forget. It was late, after 7 p.m., and I was gathering my things at the end of another long, exhausting day. Nothing felt unusual. Nothing felt spiritual. Nothing felt remarkable.

Until it did.

As I reached for my purse, a voice — clear, steady, and unmistakably God — said:

"Leave and don't come back."

I froze.

I had never heard God speak to me with such clarity.

Not in a whisper.

Not in a nudge.

This was a command.

I sat back down in my chair and said out loud, "But God... I have no backup plan."

And just as clearly, the Holy Spirit replied:

"Do you trust the creature more than the Creator?"

Those words sliced right through my logic.

I was the primary wage earner for my family.

I had a daughter in college.

A mortgage.

Bills.

Responsibility.

People depending on me.

But at that moment, none of that mattered more than obedience.

I didn't call Danny.

I didn't text a friend.

I didn't ask anyone's permission.

I didn't gather opinions.

I didn't debate or delay.

I simply obeyed.

I picked up my dad's old stress ball — my little keepsake of his strength — grabbed my purse, my notebook, and walked out of the job I had given ten years of my life to.

That was the beginning of my **pure, unfiltered walk of faith**.

A walk I did not understand.

A walk that made no earthly sense.

A walk that would later reveal the sovereign hand of God in a way that defies explanation.

Wrestling With a Generational Wound

Leaving my job was only part of the journey.

There was a deeper battle I had to face — a battle connected to grief.

My mother hid her illness from me.

She carried her suffering quietly, protecting me the only way she knew how. And although I understood her intention, her silence left me with deep emotional questions after she passed.

Questions that lingered.

Questions that hurt.

Questions God brought to the surface when I received my own diagnosis.

I said to God:

"Lord, help me not repeat the silence that wounded me. Help me to walk in honesty, not secrecy."

And He did.

He didn't allow fear or confusion to drive me into silence.

He guided me with His timing.

He covered my children.

And He redeemed what once hurt me.

This was part of the divine setup.

A Season Reserved for God

During the months between leaving my job and receiving my diagnosis, I spent more time with God than I ever had before. It was the season He used to rebuild everything inside me.

I prayed.

I journaled.

I studied Scripture.

I cried.

I listened.

I rested in His presence.

God removed the noise of my career so I could hear Him more clearly, because what was coming required spiritual sensitivity, emotional clarity, and supernatural peace.

Looking back, I now understand:

He pulled me out before the storm came so He could prepare me for it.

Divine Connections From Decades Ago

During this season, God began sending people back into my life — not random people, but believers.

A sorority sister I hadn't spoken to in **30 years** suddenly reached out.

She was a believer.

A prayer warrior.

A cancer survivor.

Then a classmate from my tiny hometown in Alabama — someone I hadn't spoken to since **1989** — reached out.

She was also a believer.

And also a cancer survivor.

God sent back women who carried **exactly** what I would need:

- Faith
- Prayer
- Understanding
- Authority
- Compassion
- Testimony

This was not coincidence.

This was orchestration.

God was building my faith circle long before I needed it.

The Rushed Diagnosis — and the Rescue

Before MD Anderson, I received a rushed diagnosis and an even more rushed treatment plan:

"We need to remove the entire breast."

"It has to be soon."

"We don't have time to wait."

It was fear-driven.

It was hurried.

It was missing something.

Had I followed that plan, I would have lost a part of my body **unnecessarily** and still not received a complete diagnosis.

But God intervened.

He whispered, *"Wait."*

And that whisper saved my life.

Because the moment I stepped into MD Anderson Cancer Center, I knew I was in the right place.

It felt like **peace**.

It felt like **order**.

It felt like **God**.

I said to myself:

"These are the people God assembled for me before the foundation of the world."

And I believe that with everything in me.

The thoroughness...

The compassion...

The patience...

The wisdom...

The attention to detail...

The discernment...

It was divine.

The Shift in My Prayer

Test after test came back **benign**.

And I celebrated each time.

But the team at MD Anderson kept saying:

"We are missing something."

They weren't panicked — they were vigilant.

They weren't rushed — they were intentional.

They weren't guessing — they were guided.

At first, my prayer was:

"Lord, please don't let them find anything."

But as I watched the team work, something changed inside me.

The prayer shifted:

"Lord, if something is there, PLEASE let them find it."

It was a surrender.

A trust.

A release of fear.

A declaration of faith.

And God honored that prayer.

The Number 7 — Completion

During the **incisional biopsy**, they removed 13 slices of tissue.

The cancer was found in the **7th cut**.

Not the 1st.

Not the 2nd.

Not the 3rd.

Not even halfway.

The **7th**.

The biblical number of **completion**.

Completion of the search.

Completion of the hidden.

Completion of the unknown.

Completion of the divine setup.

God revealed the truth

exactly where it needed to be found,

at the exact moment it needed to be discovered,

by the exact hands He had assigned to my case.

This was not luck.

This was not medicine alone.

This was **sovereignty**.

This was **protection**.

This was **God's hand**.

Every detail of my diagnosis was uncovered according to heaven's timeline.

Scripture Meditations

- **Proverbs 16:9** — "The Lord directeth his steps."
- **Romans 8:28** — "All things work together for good..."
- **Psalm 121:8** — "The Lord shall preserve thy going out..."
- **Jeremiah 1:5** — "Before I formed thee... I ordained thee."

Reflection Questions

1. Has God ever asked you to take a step without knowing the outcome?
2. How has God prepared you for battles you didn't know were coming?
3. Who has God placed in your life for such a time as this?
4. How has God revealed His sovereignty in the details of your journey?

Closing Prayer

Lord, thank You for going before me. Thank You for preparing every path, every person, every appointment, and every discovery long before I ever needed them. Help me trust Your leading even when I cannot see the full picture. Thank You for assembling the right team, for revealing what was hidden, and for completing the work You began. In Jesus' name, amen.

CHAPTER 5 — THE EMPTY PAGES BEFORE THE BREAKTHROUGH

Opening Verse

"Be still, and know that I am God."
– Psalm 46:10

Journal Entry

When this journey first began, I opened my journal with the intention of writing my way through whatever was ahead. But when I stared at those blank pages, nothing came. No words. No prayers. No thoughts I knew how to put into sentences. My heart was heavy, and my mind was overwhelmed. I felt suspended between fear and faith, unsure which direction my emotions would take me.

Those empty pages felt like a reflection of my reality — unknown, unformed, waiting to be written.

At first, the emptiness frustrated me. I thought, *If I can't even write, how am I supposed to walk through this?*

But God began showing me something deeper: the blank pages weren't emptiness… they were an invitation.

They were a place where faith could grow in silence.

A place where trust was built before the testimony.

A place where God could speak without competition.

We love the chapters of life that are full — full of answers, full of clarity, full of resolution. But no one talks about the pages before that. The quiet ones. The ones where you're waiting for results, waiting for direction, waiting for peace.

The pages that look empty... but are actually holding the weight of the breakthrough you can't yet see.

Those early days were filled with so much uncertainty. I wanted answers immediately. I wanted clarity. I wanted a plan. Instead, God told me to be still. To wait. To trust Him without knowing what He was doing behind the scenes.

And that stillness became holy ground.

In those weeks, I wrote short phrases instead of long entries. Sometimes a single scripture. Sometimes a desperate prayer like, *"Help me, Lord."* Sometimes nothing but a date — a placeholder for a moment I didn't yet understand.

Slowly, those empty pages began to fill — not with my words, but with God's presence.

Narrative Reflection

Looking back, I now see the beauty in those blank pages. They weren't evidence of weakness; they were evidence of surrender. I was giving God the space He needed to work.

Breakthrough rarely comes with noise.

It comes in the quiet.

In the stillness.

In the empty spaces we don't know how to fill.

Cancer had a name, but it didn't have the final word. Even in the silence, God was already moving. The biopsy results, the timing of my appointments, the doctors He placed in my path — everything was being aligned even when I couldn't see it.

Those blank pages became a testimony in progress.

I learned that faith grows in the in-between moments — the places where nothing seems to be happening, but God is building the foundation for what's coming. Sometimes we judge our silence as failure, but God sees it as trust.

The giants before me looked intimidating, but deep down, I believed they would fall. I didn't know how, and I didn't know when, but I sensed God whispering, *"I'm working."*

Every time I returned to my journal, the pages felt less like emptiness and more like expectation. A place where breakthrough was forming. A place where God's promises were settling into my spirit one quiet moment at a time.

Scripture Meditations

- **Habakkuk 2:3** — "Though it tarry, wait for it; because it will surely come..."
- **Psalm 27:13–14** — "Wait on the Lord: be of good courage..."
- **Lamentations 3:26** — "It is good that a man should both hope and quietly wait..."
- **Isaiah 40:31** — "They that wait upon the Lord shall renew their strength..."

Reflection Questions

1. What "blank page" moments in your life have revealed God's presence in unexpected ways?
2. How comfortable are you with waiting on God without knowing the details?
3. What might God be preparing in your silent or uncertain seasons?
4. How can you shift your view of stillness from emptiness to expectation?

Closing Prayer

Lord, thank You for reminding me that silence is not absence and emptiness is not failure. Help me trust You in the moments when I don't see the full picture. Fill my heart with peace while I wait, and let every quiet season prepare me for the breakthrough You have already planned. Teach me to rest in Your timing, knowing that You are always working for my good. In Jesus' name, amen.

Chapter 6 — The Day I Smiled

Opening Verse

"God is in the midst of her; she shall not be moved:
God shall help her, and that right early."
– Psalm 46:5

Journal Entry

On the day I heard the words *"You have breast cancer,"* something unexpected happened — I smiled. It wasn't forced. It wasn't denial. It wasn't shock. It was something deeper, something holy, something that didn't make sense in the natural.

My smile wasn't rooted in the diagnosis; it was rooted in the presence of God.

When the doctor spoke the words out loud, they seemed to float in the air for a moment, suspended between fear and faith. I remember looking at Danny, squeezing his hand, and feeling a stillness fall over the room. Not fear. Not panic. Just peace — fragile, yet undeniable.

It made no sense. Cancer is supposed to break you. It's supposed to consume your thoughts, unravel your emotions, and steal your joy. But in that moment, joy rose up inside me like a quiet rebellion against fear.

That smile was more than an expression.

It was a declaration.

A statement.

A spiritual posture.

It was the whisper of my soul saying, *"This will not move me."*

In that moment, I knew — not from my strength, but from God's — that the cancer had not come to destroy me. It had come to reveal God's glory in a way I had never experienced before.

Danny looked at me, shocked. I think part of him wondered if I understood what the doctor said. But he also saw something shift in me — something strong, something anchored, something supernatural. And that strength wasn't mine. It was God's.

That day, my smile became a memorial stone — a moment I would carry with me through every biopsy, every appointment, every sleepless night. A reminder that fear doesn't get to write my story.

Narrative Reflection

Looking back, I understand why that smile came so naturally: God's presence carries joy, even in the darkest valleys.

It wasn't the kind of joy that comes from happiness or circumstances. It was the kind of joy that only comes from knowing who walks beside you. A joy that settles deep into your spirit and says:

"Even here, even now, God is with you."

In the days that followed, that moment in the doctor's office became a reference point. When fear tried to sneak in, I remembered how God steadied me when I should have been falling apart. When doubt whispered, *"What if...?"* my spirit remembered, *"But God..."*

I realized something powerful:

Joy isn't the absence of a hard reality — it's the presence of God in the middle of it.

My smile wasn't strength; it was surrender.

It was the Holy Spirit rising in me when my flesh didn't have the ability to stand.

So many times, I returned to that moment, mentally reliving the peace that filled the room. It became evidence that God was not only with me — He was ahead of me, preparing each step.

Not one appointment surprised Him.

Not one biopsy worried Him.

Not one moment overwhelmed Him.

God was already working behind the scenes, aligning the right doctors, the right timing, and the right support system. And every time fear tried to overshadow that truth, God reminded me of the peace He gave me when I heard the diagnosis.

That peace didn't come from understanding.

It came from *trusting*.

Scripture Meditations

- **Nehemiah 8:10** — "The joy of the Lord is your strength."
- **Psalm 30:5** — "Weeping may endure for a night, but joy cometh in the morning."
- **Philippians 4:4** — "Rejoice in the Lord always…"
- **John 16:33** — "In the world ye shall have tribulation: but be of good cheer…"

Reflection Questions

1. Can you recall a moment when God gave you peace that didn't match the situation?
2. What does "joy in the midst of difficulty" look like for you?
3. How can you anchor yourself in God's presence when fear tries to rise?
4. What memorial moments has God given you that remind you of His faithfulness?

Closing Prayer

Father, thank You for the joy that strengthens me in ways I cannot explain. Thank You for meeting me in the moments when fear should have overtaken me. Let Your presence continue to fill my heart with peace that surpasses understanding. Teach me to smile through the storms, not because the storm is easy, but because You are with me every step of the way. In Jesus' name, amen.

Chapter 7 — In The Quiet

Opening Verse

"When thou passest through the waters, I will be with thee... when thou walkest through the fire, thou shalt not be burned."
– Isaiah 43:2

Journal Entry

On July 5, I woke up feeling restless. The night before had been long, filled with thoughts that kept circling around the same questions: *What now? What does this mean? What comes next?* Fear fought for space in my mind, and uncertainty pressed against my chest like a weight I couldn't push away.

Instead of turning on the TV or reaching for my phone, I sat in the quiet. No music. No noise. Just me and God. The silence at first felt uncomfortable — like I was sitting in a room with an unanswered question. But slowly, something changed. The quiet began to comfort me.

It was in that stillness that I felt God's presence wash over me like a warm blanket. Not loud. Not dramatic. Just steady. I didn't receive answers, but I received peace. And in that moment, peace was enough.

Narrative Reflection

Silence can be unsettling when your world is turned upside down. Fear thrives in the noise — in the what-ifs, the worst-case scenarios, the stories your mind tries to create. But God speaks in the quiet. When we choose stillness, we give Him room to whisper.

That morning, the quiet became my sanctuary.

It became the place where I remembered:

- God is not moved by test results.
- God is not shaken by diagnosis.
- God does His best work in the places where we stop striving and start trusting.

As the hours passed, my breathing slowed. My shoulders relaxed. And the thoughts that once raced through my mind began to settle. I learned that the quiet isn't empty — it's full of God.

That day changed the way I approached the entire journey. I learned to find God in the still moments — early mornings, late nights, pauses between appointments, times when words failed and tears spoke louder. And in each quiet moment, He met me with the same gentle assurance:

"You are Mine. You are not alone."

Scripture Meditations

- **Psalm 62:1** — "Truly my soul waiteth upon God..."
- **Philippians 4:7** — "The peace of God... shall keep your hearts and minds..."
- **Exodus 14:14** — "The Lord shall fight for you, and ye shall hold your peace."

Reflection Questions

1. How comfortable are you with silence when life feels overwhelming?

2. What might God be inviting you to hear in the quiet spaces of your day?
3. In what moments has God brought you peace without changing your circumstances?

Closing Prayer

Lord, teach me to find You in the quiet. Silence my anxious thoughts and calm my spirit. Help me trust that You are working even when I cannot see it. Let Your presence fill every still moment with peace and strength. In Jesus' name, amen.

Chapter 8 — The Comfort Of His Word

<u>Opening Verse</u>

"I sought the Lord, and he heard me, and delivered me
from all my fears."
– Psalm 34:4

<u>Journal Entry</u>

On July 6, I sat with my Bible open, needing something stronger than my own thoughts. I felt fragile that morning — like my emotions were sitting just beneath the surface, waiting to overflow. I wasn't looking for a specific verse; I just needed God to speak.

My eyes landed on Psalms 34 and 35, and as I read the words on the page, peace rose inside me. Scriptures I had read before suddenly felt alive. They weren't verses — they were nourishment. They weren't ink — they were oxygen.

God's Word became my comfort in a way I had never experienced before.

<u>Narrative Reflection</u>

During a journey like this, your mind becomes loud — louder than your faith at times. Doubts, fears, unknowns... they cloud your thinking. But Scripture cuts through all of it like light in a dark room.

God began using His Word to steady me:

- A verse would calm my anxiety.
- A promise would silence a lie.
- A psalm would remind me who He is.
- A story would remind me what He's capable of.

I started writing verses on sticky notes and placing them around the house. On mirrors. In my journal. In my car. Each time I felt fear rising, I read one out loud. And the more I spoke His Word, the more my spirit aligned with truth.

God wasn't just speaking to me — He was guarding me.

His Word became my shield:

- When my thoughts raced, Scripture slowed them.
- When fear whispered, Scripture shouted louder.
- When uncertainty came, Scripture reminded me of God's sovereignty.

That morning taught me something beautiful:

When you cannot feel God, read His Word — because His Word carries His presence.

Scripture Meditations

- **Hebrews 4:12** — "The word of God is quick, and powerful…"
- **Joshua 1:9** — "Be strong and of a good courage…"
- **Psalm 119:105** — "Thy word is a lamp unto my feet…"

Reflection Questions

1. What scriptures bring comfort when fear rises in your life?
2. How can you incorporate God's Word into your daily routine more intentionally?
3. Which of God's promises anchor you in seasons of uncertainty?

Closing Prayer

Lord, thank You for the power of Your Word. Let it strengthen me, ground me, and guard my heart from fear. Fill my mind with Your promises and help me cling to Your truth when uncertainty tries to overwhelm me. In Jesus' name, amen.

CHAPTER 9 — ALL THINGS FOR GOOD

Opening Verse

*"And we know that all things work together for good
to them that love God..."*
– Romans 8:28

Journal Entry

On July 6, I began noticing something beautiful — God was revealing Himself not only in the big moments, but in the small ones. A text message at just the right time. A prayer from someone I hadn't spoken to in years. A word of encouragement that landed in my heart exactly when I needed it.

But what truly amazed me was who God used.

One by one, **believers** began reaching out — people I hadn't seen in decades.

My sorority sister — someone I hadn't connected with in over 30 years — messaged me out of nowhere. A woman of faith. A cancer survivor. A prayer warrior.

Then a high school classmate from my tiny hometown in Alabama reached out. Someone I hadn't spoken to since 1989. She too was a believer... and a cancer survivor.

Neither of them knew what I was facing.

Neither knew I needed encouragement.

But God did.

Narrative Reflection

Their messages weren't casual. They were divine appointments.

They prayed with me.

They prayed for me.

They shared scriptures that had strengthened them.

They reminded me that God was still working.

They spoke faith, not fear.

These reconnections were evidence of Romans 8:28 in motion.

God was weaving together people, timing, and testimonies long before I understood why.

Not every voice brought comfort. Some meant well, but their words carried fear instead of faith. God taught me to guard my spirit — to close the door gently but firmly on anything that stirred anxiety.

The voices He sent carried peace.

They carried hope.

They carried authority — because they had survived what I was just beginning.

Each conversation became a reminder that **God sees details we overlook.**

Nothing in my journey was random.

Nothing was wasted.

Nothing caught Him off guard.

God was building my circle before the battle began.

He was showing me that if He could orchestrate these connections from decades ago, then surely He could orchestrate my healing, my steps, my peace, and my future.

Romans 8:28 became more than a verse — it became my reality.

All things — even old friendships, unexpected messages, and quiet prayers — were working for my good.

Scripture Meditations

- **Psalm 121:8** — "The Lord shall preserve thy going out..."
- **Isaiah 46:4** — "Even to old age... I will carry you."
- **Psalm 34:4** — "He delivered me from all my fears."

Reflection Questions

1. Who has God brought back into your life as a source of strength or encouragement?
2. How have unexpected voices spoken faith into your journey?
3. What does Romans 8:28 mean to you in your current season?

Closing Prayer

Lord, thank You for the way You orchestrate every detail of my life. Thank You for surrounding me with believers who speak faith, hope, and truth. Help me discern the voices that strengthen my spirit and gently shut out the ones that do not. Let me see Your hand in every connection, every moment, and every blessing. In Jesus' name, amen.

Part II - The Healing & Revelation

✺ Chapter 10 — Message From My Mother: Still Connected

Opening Verse

"I will not leave you comfortless: I will come to you."
– John 14:18

Journal Entry

This week, God reminded me of something tender and sacred — that love does not end, and neither does the influence of those who walked with Christ before us. I found a message my mother had written years before she passed. A simple note. A few words. But the timing of discovering it was nothing short of divine.

She had been gone since 2022, yet here she was — speaking to me in the season when I needed her voice most. Tears filled my eyes as I read her handwriting, hearing her heart in every stroke of the pen. It felt as though God had preserved that message specifically for this moment, waiting until I would need the comfort of her words.

I realized that my mother had been preparing me for this long before I knew I would walk this road.

Narrative Reflection

Grief has a way of convincing us that connection ends with death. But faith tells a different story. When someone walks closely with God, the imprint of their love doesn't disappear — it lingers, covers, strengthens, and continues to guide.

My mother's message wasn't just sentimental; it was a spiritual reminder that the prayers she prayed over me are still active. Her intercession didn't die with her body. Her legacy didn't fade with time. Her voice still encourages me, her faith still influences me, and her love still wraps around me in ways only God could orchestrate.

In the hardest moments of this journey, God allowed me to feel her nearness — not physically, but spiritually. Her message reminded me that heaven watches, heaven comforts, and heaven participates in ways we cannot always see.

I realized that God often uses the legacy of our loved ones to reassure us of His presence. Just as He promised not to leave us comfortless, He often sends reminders through memories, words, and signs that are too perfect to be coincidence.

Her words were a reminder that I was not walking alone — I was walking covered.

Scripture Meditations

- **2 Timothy 1:5** — "The unfeigned faith... dwelt first in thy grandmother... and thy mother..."
- **Hebrews 12:1** — "We are surrounded by so great a cloud of witnesses..."
- **Psalm 116:15** — "Precious in the sight of the Lord is the death of his saints."

Reflection Questions

1. How has God used memories or messages from loved ones to comfort you?
2. What spiritual legacy has been passed down to you through your family?
3. How can you honor the prayers and faith of those who came before you?

<u>Closing Prayer</u>

Lord, thank You for the love and legacy of those who walked with You before me. Thank You for sending reminders of their presence and their prayers when I need them most. Let their faith continue through me, and let their legacy strengthen my walk with You. In Jesus' name, amen.

Chapter 11 — She's Still On My Right Side

Opening Verse

"He shall cover thee with his feathers, and under his wings shalt thou trust..."
– Psalm 91:4

Journal Entry

On July 8, I found myself looking through old photographs of my mother and me. I wasn't searching for anything specific — just allowing memories to wash over me. But then I noticed something I had never seen before.

In almost every photo of us together, my mother was resting her head on my **right side** — the same breast where the cancer was later found.

It stopped me in my tracks.

What I had once seen as a casual pose suddenly felt intentional, prophetic, almost sacred. It was as if God was showing me that she had been covering me long before I ever needed the covering.

Narrative Reflection

There are moments in life when God pulls back the curtain just enough for us to see His tenderness. This was one of those moments.

My mother was a nurse — calm, steady, gentle, and full of

wisdom. If she were still alive, she would have been beside me at every appointment, translating medical language into comfort. She would have been my calm in the chaos.

But instead, God allowed me to feel her presence in a different way. Those photographs became a love letter — a message from both heaven and God's heart, saying, *"You were covered then. You are covered now."*

I realized something beautiful:

When people of faith leave this earth, the influence of their prayers doesn't leave with them.

Every time I looked at those photos, peace washed over me. Not the kind of peace that comes from logic, but the kind that comes from God — deep, warm, and undeniable.

It reminded me that grief does not diminish connection.

Love doesn't evaporate because a heartbeat stops.

And faith doesn't end when a body is buried.

My mother's faith lived on through me. And in those pictures, God showed me that her love had been positioned exactly where my battle would be — my right side.

Scripture Meditations

- **John 14:18** — "I will not leave you comfortless..."
- **Psalm 23:6** — "Surely goodness and mercy shall follow me..."
- **Psalm 91:11** — "He shall give His angels charge over thee..."

Reflection Questions

1. What reminders of love or protection has God shown you during your journey?
2. How do you see the faith of loved ones reflected in your own life today?

3. What comfort has God given you through memories or unexpected signs?

<u>Closing Prayer</u>

Father, thank You for the reminders that I am covered — by Your love, by Your presence, and by the legacy of those who loved You. Let these reminders strengthen me, comfort me, and keep me grounded in Your faithfulness. In Jesus' name, amen.

❧ CHAPTER 12 — A MESSAGE TO ❧ MY FUTURE SELF

Opening Verse

"Who comforteth us in all our tribulation, that we may be able to comfort them which are in any trouble..."
– 2 Corinthians 1:4

Journal Entry

As I sat with my journal one afternoon, I felt the Holy Spirit prompting me to write — not to the present version of myself, but to the *future* me. At first, it felt unusual. Why write to someone I hadn't become yet? But the nudge was strong, so I obeyed.

I wrote these words to the woman I would one day become after the storm:

"One day, you will tell your story of how you overcame, and it will be someone else's survival guide."

I didn't realize it then, but that sentence was prophetic. It was God speaking to my future, reassuring me that everything I was facing would serve a purpose far greater than fear or diagnosis.

Narrative Reflection

Writing to my future self gave me courage. It forced me to imagine a day beyond the valley — a day when healing wasn't a hope, but a reality. It allowed me to see myself standing on the other side, looking back not with trauma, but with testimony.

I realized that my pain wasn't isolated — it was connected to someone else's breakthrough.

My battle wasn't wasted — it would become someone else's roadmap.

My faith wasn't private — it would one day strengthen others.

Pain becomes powerful when it becomes purpose.

God whispered to my heart that the woman who was trembling today would be a warrior tomorrow. And the words I wrote to her would become a bridge between those two versions of me.

Every trial I endured, every fear I confronted, every tear I cried — all of it would one day stand as evidence that God carries His children through the darkest valleys and leads them into light.

Writing to my future self wasn't just therapeutic —

it was warfare.

It was declaring victory before I saw it.

It was speaking life into a future that fear wanted to steal.

It was aligning my words with God's promises rather than my emotions.

And now, living in the answered prayer of that future, I understand why God told me to write it:

He wanted me to know that healing was not only possible — it was promised.

Scripture Meditations

- **Romans 8:18** — "The sufferings of this present time are not worthy..."
- **Revelation 12:11** — "They overcame... by the word of their testimony..."
- **Isaiah 43:19** — "Behold, I will do a new thing..."

Reflection Questions

1. If you were to write a message to your future self today, what would it say?
2. How might your current challenges become someone else's testimony of hope?
3. What victory do you need to declare in advance?

Closing Prayer

Lord, thank You for reminding me that my story is not just for me — it is for others who will walk through their own valley. Give me the courage to speak life over my future and to believe that You are already working all things for good. Let my testimony become a light for others. In Jesus' name, amen.

CHAPTER 13 — SCRIPTURES IN THE SILENCE

Opening Verse

"And after the earthquake a fire; but the Lord was not in the fire: and after the fire a still small voice."
— 1 Kings 19:12

Journal Entry

There came a moment in this journey when I realized that the loudest part of fear wasn't the diagnosis — it was the silence that followed. The quiet space between appointments. The stillness between one test and the next. The gaps where no answers existed yet.

Those silent places can feel dangerous if you're not careful. Your mind wants to fill them with "what ifs," with dread, with imagination. But I sensed God inviting me to do something different. To sit in the silence and let Him speak.

One morning, I opened my journal and forced myself not to rush, not to think, not to scroll, not to distract myself — just to wait. I sat with my pen in hand and whispered, *"Lord, whatever Scripture You bring to my mind, I will write it down."*

And then I waited.

Slowly — gently — Scriptures began rising in my spirit like waves rolling onto shore.

"Fear thou not; for I am with thee..."

"The Lord is my shepherd..."
"I will never leave thee nor forsake thee..."
"Be still, and know that I am God."

Each verse came like a breath of fresh air. Not random. Not forced. Just truth bubbling up from places God had planted long ago. I realized those Scriptures had been inside me for years — waiting for this moment to come alive.

Narrative Reflection

That day, Scripture became my shelter.

It wasn't that God suddenly answered every question. It wasn't that fear disappeared instantly. It wasn't that the diagnosis changed. But the **atmosphere** inside me shifted.

Scripture has a way of doing that — of filling silence with certainty, filling emptiness with truth, filling fear with light.

I learned something powerful about God in that season:

He is a God who speaks in whispers.

He doesn't compete with noise.

He doesn't push.

He doesn't shout.

He waits for your spirit to quiet long enough for His Word to rise.

And when it rises, it brings peace that doesn't make sense.

There were Scriptures I hadn't read in months — some I hadn't thought of in years — and yet they surfaced right when I needed them. Verses about protection, about peace, about healing, about God's faithfulness.

It reminded me that His Word never leaves us. Even when we feel empty, His Word is full. Even when we feel weak, His Word is strong. Even when we don't know what to pray, His Word prays for us.

I realized that Scripture doesn't just comfort —

It corrects.

It anchors.

It reassures.

It fights for you when you're too tired to fight for yourself.

And it taught me that silent seasons aren't empty seasons. They're sacred. They're the places where His Word becomes *personal*. Where verses become lifelines. Where the Bible stops being a book and becomes a voice.

God wasn't asking me to fill the silence.

He was asking me to **listen** in it.

Scripture Meditations

- **Psalm 119:105** — "Thy word is a lamp unto my feet, and a light unto my path."
- **Isaiah 55:11** — "So shall my word be... it shall accomplish that which I please."
- **Hebrews 4:12** — "The word of God is quick, and powerful..."
- **Psalm 1:2–3** — "His delight is in the law of the Lord... and he shall be like a tree planted..."

Reflection Questions

1. What Scriptures rise in your heart when you are quiet enough to listen?
2. How do you respond to silence — with fear, distraction, or openness to God's voice?
3. What would change if you allowed Scripture to fill the silent places of your life?
4. When has God spoken to you through His Word in a way you couldn't ignore?

Closing Prayer

Lord, thank You for speaking through Your Word when everything around me feels quiet and uncertain. Teach me to treasure the silent moments, to lean into them, and to trust that You are speaking even when I cannot see the full picture. Fill my mind and my heart with Your truth, and let Your Word bring peace to every place where fear tries to settle. In Jesus' name, amen.

CHAPTER 14 — A DIVINE CALL FROM MY SORORITY SISTER

Opening Verse

"Wherefore comfort yourselves together, and edify one another, even as also ye do."
— 1 Thessalonians 5:11

Journal Entry

One afternoon, in the middle of the waiting, fear, and emotional exhaustion that comes with a diagnosis, my phone rang. The name that appeared on my screen stunned me — it was my sorority sister, someone I hadn't seen or spoken to in over thirty years.

Thirty years.

Three decades.

A lifetime of distance.

We hadn't stayed in touch. We weren't social-media close. We weren't "check in every year" friends. We were women whose lives had gone in completely different directions. And yet, on that day — that exact moment — she called me.

As soon as I heard her voice, something inside me softened. There was familiarity there, history there, but also something deeper — assignment.

Before I could even explain what I was going through, she said, "Kim... God put you on my heart."

It wasn't casual.

It wasn't coincidence.

It was divine.

Narrative Reflection

As we talked, I quickly learned that she, too, had walked her own valley — she was a cancer survivor. A believer. A woman whose faith had been tested and strengthened. A woman who knew what spiritual warfare felt like. A woman who knew how to pray.

She didn't call to share fear or horror stories. She didn't say, "I knew someone who..." or "You better be careful..."

No.

She came with faith.

She came with compassion.

She came with **spiritual authority**.

She prayed with me.

She prayed *over* me.

She prayed *through* me.

Words I didn't have strength to pray for myself rolled off her tongue with power and peace.

There is something deeply comforting about being prayed for by someone who has lived the testimony you are still waiting for. She didn't just understand the journey — she had survived it. She had found God in the fire. And she was calling to lead me through mine.

Throughout our conversation, I felt the presence of God settle into the room. Her voice carried the strength of someone who had fought fear and won. Her words were seasoned with Scripture, soaked in hope, and anchored in truth. She spoke to me the way only a seasoned believer can — gently, boldly, confidently.

She reminded me to keep my spiritual guard up.

To filter every voice.

To shut out noise rooted in fear, even if it came from good intentions.

To stand firm in the Word.

To expect God's hand to move.

To protect my peace like it was sacred — because it was.

And then she said something that pierced me straight to my core:

"Kim, you are not fighting this alone. God has already gone before you."

Those words wrapped around me like armor.

This was no ordinary phone call.

This was a lifeline.

This was reinforcement.

This was God sending someone who carried exactly what I needed in that moment.

I hung up the phone with tears streaming down my face — tears of relief, gratitude, and awe. How could a woman I hadn't spoken to since college show up at the exact moment I needed encouragement?

Because **God sent her**.

This is how He works.

He sends the right people at the right time with the right words.

Not by accident.

Not by coincidence.

By divine alignment.

That call became a turning point. It strengthened my spirit, reminded me of God's faithfulness, and confirmed that heaven was paying attention. It felt like God whispering, *"I see you. I'm with you. I have already assigned people to help carry you through this."*

Her obedience became my strength.

Her testimony became my hope.

Her prayer became my peace.

Scripture Meditations

- **Galatians 6:2** — "Bear ye one another's burdens..."
- **Proverbs 27:17** — "Iron sharpeneth iron..."
- **Hebrews 10:24** — "Let us consider one another to provoke unto love and good works..."

<u>Reflection Questions</u>

1. Has God ever sent someone into your life at exactly the right moment?
2. What faith-filled voices has God placed around you for strength and encouragement?
3. How can you discern the difference between voices rooted in fear and voices rooted in faith?
4. Who might God be calling *you* to encourage today?

<u>Closing Prayer</u>

Lord, thank You for the divine connections You place in my life. Thank You for sending people who carry Your truth, Your encouragement, and Your strength. Help me recognize the voices that speak faith and gently distance myself from those rooted in fear. Use me, Lord, to be a source of comfort and hope to others just as You have sent others to comfort me. In Jesus' name, amen.

Chapter 15 — Faith Over Fear

Opening Verse

"Fear thou not; for I am with thee: be not dismayed;
for I am thy God: I will strengthen thee; yea, I will
help thee..."
– Isaiah 41:10

Journal Entry

Fear is a strange companion. It doesn't need an invitation — it just shows up. It creeps into quiet moments, whispers in the back of your mind, and tries to attach itself to every thought. After my simulation for radiation, fear tried to make itself at home in my spirit.

I remember lying on the table as they positioned my body and marked my skin. The machine hovered above me, the lights felt cold and clinical, and the reality of my diagnosis pressed against my chest like a weight. I felt small. Vulnerable. Exposed.

For a moment, fear got louder than my faith.

When I got home that evening, I could feel the heaviness of it. My emotions were tangled — part of me wanted to cry, part of me wanted to pretend everything was fine, and part of me just wanted to crawl into God's arms and stay there.

Before bed, I whispered, *"Lord, I need You."* I didn't have strength for anything more. I didn't know what to pray. I didn't know how to feel. All I knew was I needed Him.

And God — being the loving Father He is — met me right where I was.

Narrative Reflection

That night, and again the next morning, God took me back through my journey — step by step — reminding me of every single place He had carried me.

The whisper that pushed me to go to the mammogram.

The butterfly that appeared before my biopsy.

The cardinal before surgery.

The sorority sister who called out of nowhere.

The high school classmate I hadn't spoken to since 1989.

The believers He surrounded me with.

The peace that settled in the doctor's office on diagnosis day.

The way fear had tried before and failed every single time.

As I replayed these moments, something shifted in me.

Fear loosened its grip.

Faith rose up with new strength.

And I heard the Holy Spirit whisper, *"You've already seen My faithfulness. Why fear now?"*

Faith over fear wasn't a slogan for me — it was survival.

It was spiritual warfare.

It was choosing, moment by moment, to believe God's character more than my circumstances.

I realized that fear wants attention. It wants you to replay worst-case scenarios. It wants you to magnify uncertainty. But faith invites you to look at God's track record. Faith invites you to remember every miracle, every whisper, every answered prayer, every moment God did what only He could do.

Fear exaggerates.

Faith remembers.

Fear shouts.

Faith stands.

Fear tries to dictate your story.

Faith declares who writes it.

That morning, strength returned to my spirit. Not because anything got easier, but because I remembered who was fighting for me. And when God fights for you, fear is always outnumbered.

Faith over fear became my daily decision — not just in the big moments, but in the small ones. Every time anxiety rose, I reminded myself:

"God has been faithful every step of this journey. He will be faithful in this one too."

Scripture Meditations

- **2 Timothy 1:7** — "For God hath not given us the spirit of fear..."
- **Psalm 56:3** — "What time I am afraid, I will trust in thee."
- **Joshua 1:9** — "Be strong and of a good courage..."
- **Psalm 46:1** — "God is our refuge and strength, a very present help..."

Reflection Questions

1. What moments of God's past faithfulness can you bring to mind when fear rises?
2. How does fear try to speak to you — and how can you answer it with truth?
3. What would choosing faith over fear look like in your current season?
4. What spiritual "evidence" has God shown you that He is with you?

Closing Prayer

Lord, thank You for being greater than every fear that tries to rise against my spirit. Thank You for reminding me of ev-

ery moment You carried me, protected me, comforted me, and strengthened me. Teach me to choose faith when fear whispers lies. Let Your promises silence every anxious thought. I trust You with every step ahead, knowing that You go before me and stand beside me. In Jesus' name, amen.

CHAPTER 16 — LITE UP THE WORLD

Opening Verse

"Ye are the light of the world. A city that is set on a hill cannot be hid."
– Matthew 5:14

Journal Entry

On the morning of my second lumpectomy — July 26, 2025 — God spoke to me in a way I will never forget. I woke up heavy, not from fear, but from the weight of everything I had been walking through. It was a different kind of morning. Quiet. Holy. Sacred.

Before the sun came up, I went outside to pray. The air was still. The world seemed paused, as if holding its breath. And as I stood there, asking God for peace, direction, and strength, a bright red cardinal landed on my fence.

It didn't flinch.

It didn't move.

It just stared at me.

My breath caught in my chest.

My father always used to say, *"I know... it's gonna be alright,"* whenever I was scared, stressed, or overwhelmed. It was his way of calming me, of bringing me back to center. And seeing that cardinal — his color, his presence, his stillness — felt like hearing my father say those words again, right when I needed them most.

I whispered, *"Thank You, Lord."*

I knew this was a sign — a reminder that heaven was closer than I realized.

But God wasn't finished speaking.

That same morning, I had a dream. In it, I saw three words written in big, bright letters:

"Lite up the world."

At first, I didn't understand why it was spelled *lite* and not *light*. But then the Holy Spirit whispered:

"It's not about how bright or perfect you are... it's about the glow you carry from Me."

In that moment, I knew exactly what God was saying:

My purpose wasn't about striving.

It wasn't about performing.

It wasn't about being strong, loud, or flawless.

My purpose was to shine — softly, faithfully — exactly as God created me.

Not by force.

Not by effort.

But by presence.

By walking with Him.

By trusting Him.

By reflecting Him.

That morning, before I ever stepped foot into the hospital, God gave me my assignment:

Shine where you are.

Shine as you are.

Shine because I am with you.

Narrative Reflection

As I prepared for surgery, the dream replayed over and over in my mind. "Lite up the world." The more I thought about it, the more I realized how much pressure we put on ourselves to be perfect before we shine — to have everything together, to feel strong, to be qualified, to not be afraid.

But God doesn't call the perfect.

He calls the willing.

He doesn't ask for brilliance — just obedience.

He doesn't require extraordinary — just availability.

In the season of my greatest weakness, God revealed a purpose I never expected:

My healing would become my glow.

My testimony would become my light.

I walked into the hospital that morning not just for surgery, but with a renewed sense of identity. I wasn't a victim. I wasn't weak. I wasn't fragile. I was chosen. I was covered. I was loved. I was called.

And I would shine — not because everything was perfect, but because God was present.

The beauty of "lite" is that it's simple. Soft. Gentle. Accessible. It reminds me that sometimes the most powerful ministry comes from simply being who God made you to be — scars, tears, and all.

You shine when you encourage someone who's hurting.

You shine when you pray for someone silently.

You shine when you show kindness in a harsh world.

You shine when you tell your story without shame.

You shine when you stay faithful in the valley.

That dream became a defining moment in my journey.

It wasn't just a message — it was a mandate.

God was saying:

"You are light because My light is in you —

and no darkness can put it out."

Scripture Meditations

- **Philippians 2:15** — "Among whom ye shine as lights in the world."
- **John 1:5** — "The light shineth in darkness; and the darkness comprehended it not."
- **Isaiah 60:1** — "Arise, shine; for thy light is come..."

Reflection Questions

1. What has God asked you to "shine" through, even when it didn't feel comfortable?
2. When has God used your weakness or vulnerability to reflect His glory?
3. How can you "lite up the world" in simple, everyday ways?

Closing Prayer

Lord, thank You for reminding me that I do not have to be perfect to shine. Your light in me is enough. Teach me to shine softly, faithfully, and courageously wherever You place me. Let my story reflect Your goodness and let my presence bring hope to others. Make me a vessel of Your light in every room I enter. In Jesus' name, amen.

CHAPTER 17 — SILENT TIME WITH GOD

Opening Verse

"But seek ye first the kingdom of God, and his righteousness; and all these things shall be added unto you."
– Matthew 6:33

Journal Entry

In the middle of everything — the diagnosis, the appointments, the phone calls, the quiet fears I didn't always speak out loud — I began longing for time alone with God in a way I never had before. Not rushed prayers. Not quick devotionals. Not reading a verse here or there and moving on.

I needed silence.

I needed stillness.

I needed Him.

There were days when I didn't have words left to pray. Days when my heart was heavy, but my spirit felt numb. Days when the world felt too loud and too fast. So I started making time for God the same way I made time for doctor visits — intentionally, consistently, urgently.

One morning, I sat in silence before God. No music. No journal. No requests. Just presence.

And in that silence, something inside me shifted.

Narrative Reflection

Silent time with God isn't popular in a world that celebrates noise. We fill our days with notifications, conversations, responsibilities, and distractions. But I learned in this season that silence is sacred — and silence is spiritual strength.

When I sat quietly before God, I didn't hear audible words. I didn't see visions. I didn't feel fireworks or dramatic revelation. What I felt was peace — deep, grounding, unexplainable peace.

It was the kind of peace that doesn't make sense in the middle of uncertainty.

The kind that wraps around your chest and slows your breathing.

The kind that whispers, *"You're safe here."*

That silence became my sanctuary.

In the quiet, I found:

- **Clarity** I didn't know I needed
- **Comfort** I couldn't have created on my own
- **Strength** that didn't feel like mine
- **Answers** that came not in words but in peace

There were moments in that silence when God reminded me of Scriptures I hadn't read in months. Verses would float into my mind, one after another, like breadcrumbs leading me back to His heart. I realized the Holy Spirit wasn't silent — I had just been too busy to hear Him.

The silence taught me something precious:

Sometimes the most powerful worship is not sung — it's surrendered.

I felt myself being rebuilt from the inside out.

God wasn't just healing my body — He was healing parts of my heart I didn't know were wounded.

He was restoring what the busyness of life had taken.

He was reminding me who I was and whose I was.

In the stillness, I became aware of God in every small detail —

the sunlight through my window, the quiet hum of the house, the sound of my own breathing. Every moment whispered one truth:

"I am here."

And when you truly know God is there, silence becomes sweet instead of scary.

Scripture Meditations

- **Psalm 46:10** — "Be still, and know that I am God."
- **Lamentations 3:26** — "It is good... to quietly wait for the salvation of the Lord."
- **Isaiah 30:15** — "In quietness and in confidence shall be your strength."

Reflection Questions

1. When was the last time you sat in silence with God without asking for anything?
2. What distractions might God be asking you to lay aside so you can hear Him more clearly?
3. How does silence make you feel — anxious, peaceful, or somewhere in between?
4. What might God want to reveal to you in unhurried, quiet moments?

Closing Prayer

Lord, thank You for meeting me in the stillness. Teach me to slow down, to quiet my mind, and to listen for Your whisper. Remove the distractions that compete for my attention and draw me deeper into Your presence. Let my silent time with You strengthen my faith, anchor my heart, and remind me that You are always near. In Jesus' name, amen.

PART III — THE TESTIMONY & TRANSFORMATION

 # CHAPTER 18 — TELLING THE KIDS

Opening Verse

"I have no greater joy than to hear that my children walk in truth."
— 3 John 1:4

Journal Entry

Twenty-eight days after my diagnosis, I finally sat down with Zachary and Madison to tell them what I had been walking through. Those twenty-eight days carried more weight than even the diagnosis itself — because I wasn't just holding a medical truth, I was holding a mother's responsibility.

I wanted to protect them.

I wanted to guard their peace.

I wanted to make sure fear didn't reach their hearts before faith did.

And I prayed every day for God to show me when and how to speak.

Before I could tell them anything, I had to wrestle with a part of my own story — a wound from my past that God gently brought to the surface.

My mother hid her illness from me.

She didn't tell me how serious things were until her body could no longer hide the truth. She carried her suffering quietly, wanting to shield me. And part of me understood why — mothers bear their children's pain as if it's their own, so it feels natural to try to spare them.

But another part of me grieved the silence.

I had to live through the shock of finding out too late.

I had to navigate confusion, hurt, and unanswered questions.

I mourned not just her passing, but the time I didn't know I was losing.

So when I received my diagnosis, a fear rose in me — not of cancer, but of repeating a generational pattern. I cried out to God:

"Lord, help me NOT to wound my children with silence. Help me do this differently than what hurt me."

In our household, we value transparency.

We value truth.

We value communication that strengthens connection.

But I didn't want to tell them too early, when all we had was uncertainty. I didn't want to give fear a head start. I didn't want to plant seeds of worry in hearts that were still healing from their own losses.

Especially Madison.

Her favorite great-aunt — someone she adored and looked up to — died from breast cancer. That loss shaped her understanding of the word. For Madison, "cancer" wasn't a medical term — it was trauma.

She associated the word with death, grief, and fear.

So I prayed an extra prayer over her:

"God, protect her heart.

Prepare her mind.

Let her hear this news under Your peace, not fear."

And God answered that prayer in the most beautiful, tender way possible.

Narrative Reflection

On the morning of August 3, God whispered to me, *"Today."*

And as soon as He said it, I knew why.

By the time He asked me to speak...

I was already **cancer free.**

Only God could orchestrate that kind of mercy.

Only God could protect my daughter's heart by letting the testimony be louder than the diagnosis.

Only God could redeem a generational wound by allowing my children to hear:

Not "I have cancer,"

but **"The cancer is gone."**

Not fear,

but **victory.**

Not uncertainty,

but **God's faithfulness.**

When we finally sat down, Zachary and Madison could sense something serious was coming. They could read it on my face, feel it in the room. Children — even adult children — have a way of sensing the atmosphere before the words ever arrive.

I took a deep breath and spoke with the calmness that only came from God:

"I was diagnosed with Stage zero breast cancer...

but God has already taken care of it.

The cancer is gone."

Madison's eyes immediately filled with tears, but they weren't the kind I feared. They weren't rooted in devastation — they were rooted in relief.

She leaned into me and whispered, "Mom... God really carried you."

And in that moment, I felt the Holy Spirit whisper back to my heart:

"I carried her, too."

Zachary nodded slowly, his shoulders settling as he exhaled the breath he didn't realize he was holding. "If God brought you through this," he said, "He's not done writing your story."

Their responses told me everything.

Fear had not entered the room.
Faith had.
And God showed me something profound:
Parents don't protect their children by hiding truth.
They protect their children by living truth.
By showing them what faith looks like in the valley.
By revealing God's strength when their own runs out.
In that moment, something healed inside me — not just my body, but my heart.
I realized I had broken a generational cycle.
I had given my children what I once needed:
truth, timing, safety, and God's presence.
That day did not divide us — it united us.
It did not create fear — it built faith.
It did not weaken my children — it strengthened them.
Telling them was not the end of a journey.
It was the beginning of a legacy.

Scripture Meditations

- **Isaiah 54:13** — "All thy children shall be taught of the Lord..."
- **Psalm 112:7** — "He shall not be afraid of evil tidings..."
- **Proverbs 3:3–4** — "Let not mercy and truth forsake thee..."
- **Psalm 34:4** — "He delivered me from all my fears."

Reflection Questions

1. What difficult truths has God helped you share with those you love?
2. How has God redeemed or healed communication patterns in your family line?
3. What legacy of faith do you want your children to inherit from you?

4. How has God protected your family's hearts through His timing?

<u>Closing Prayer</u>

Lord, thank You for the way You protected Zachary and Madison's hearts. Thank You for redeeming what hurt me in my past and allowing honesty, transparency, and healing to flow through our home. Thank You for the timing, the victory, and the peace You provided before I ever spoke a word. Help me continue to lead my children with faith, courage, and truth. Cover them all the days of their lives. In Jesus' name, amen.

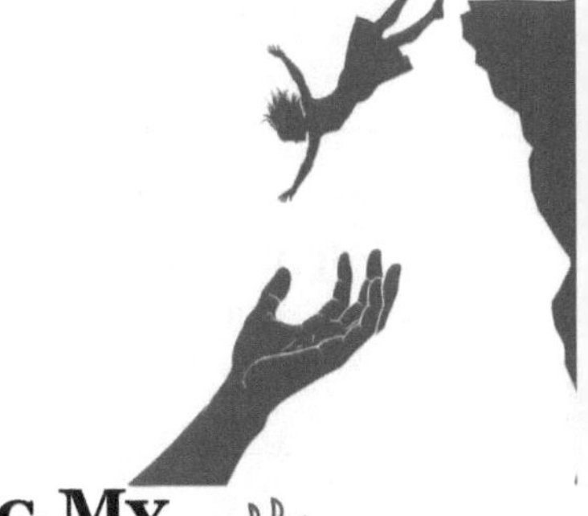

CHAPTER 19 — GUARDING MY CIRCLE

"Keep thy heart with all diligence; for out of it are the issues of life."
– Proverbs 4:23

Journal Entry

As I walked through this journey, one truth became clearer than ever:

I had to guard my circle.

Not everyone could walk with me.

Not every voice deserved access to my heart.

Not every opinion carried faith.

Cancer has a way of exposing people — what they believe, how they love, how they respond under pressure. It reveals who can stand in the gap for you and who unintentionally pulls you into fear.

I realized early on that protecting my spirit was just as important as protecting my body.

I needed people who could pray, not panic.

Encourage, not overwhelm.

Speak life, not fear.

Hold confidence, not confusion.

Some people meant well, but their words carried anxiety instead of peace. Their stories were rooted in trauma, not testimonies. Their tone was full of concern but empty of faith.

And in a season where my heart felt tender and vulnerable, my spirit simply could not afford that.

Narrative Reflection

God taught me something powerful: **love everyone — but guard your access.**

Not everyone who loves you is equipped to speak into your valley.

Not everyone who cares about you carries faith.

Not everyone who reaches out should be allowed to shape your emotions.

Some people bring fear wrapped in love.

Others bring peace wrapped in truth.

I had to discern the difference.

God began highlighting the voices that were safe for this season — voices rooted in Scripture, anchored in prayer, and grounded in spiritual maturity.

These were the ones who strengthened me:

- The ones who prayed with authority.
- The ones who reminded me of God's promises—not worst-case scenarios.
- The ones who spoke healing, not horror stories.
- The ones who didn't shrink back from the word "cancer," but elevated the word "God."
- The ones who carried the type of peace that calms storms.

These were the voices God assigned to me.

And then there were others — people I love deeply — but who unintentionally introduced fear. Not because they wanted to hurt me, but because they didn't know how to carry this kind of battle. Their words, though sincere, planted seeds I had to uproot later.

Some said, "My coworker had that... and it spread."

Others said, "You need to get prepared for..."

Or, "They say those things can come back."

I know they cared. But their words weren't for me.

Not for this season.

Not for this battle.

Not for this journey.

God was teaching me to filter everything through His Spirit:

Does this voice make my faith rise?

Or does it make my fear rise?

If it brought peace — I welcomed it.

If it brought fear — I closed the door.

Not in anger.

Not in offense.

But in wisdom.

Guarding my circle wasn't about shutting people out — it was about keeping my heart protected.

Discernment Moments

During this season, I noticed something unexpected:

The people God sent back into my life after decades were faith-filled warriors.

And the people who were immediately closest to me — though loving — sometimes didn't have the strength required for this battle.

God used far-away voices to speak near to my heart.

Voices I hadn't heard in decades.

Voices He handpicked for such a time as this.

My faith circle wasn't determined by proximity — it was determined by purpose.

Some people in my life were assigned to comfort me.

Others were assigned to intercede for me.

Others were assigned simply to listen.

And some — as much as I loved them — were not assigned to this part of the journey at all.

Learning that set me free.

Scripture Meditations

- **1 Corinthians 15:33** — "Evil communications corrupt good manners."
- **Proverbs 13:20** — "He that walketh with wise men shall be wise..."
- **Psalm 1:1–3** — "Blessed is the man that walketh not in the counsel of the ungodly..."

Reflection Questions

1. Who in your life speaks faith, peace, and truth into your journey?
2. Are there voices you need to gently distance yourself from in order to guard your heart?
3. What qualities do you look for in people who speak into your spirit during difficult seasons?
4. How can you discern which relationships are *assigned* to your journey?

Closing Prayer

Lord, thank You for teaching me how to guard my heart with wisdom and grace. Show me clearly the voices that You have assigned to strengthen me, and help me lovingly distance myself from anything that brings fear instead of faith. Surround me with people who speak life, truth, courage, and peace. Protect my spirit and anchor my heart in Your voice above all others. In Jesus' name, amen.

CHAPTER 20 — DAY 28: CANCER-FREE

Opening Verse

"This is the Lord's doing; it is marvellous in our eyes."
— Psalm 118:23

Journal Entry

Exactly twenty-eight days after hearing the words *"You have breast cancer,"* I heard a new set of words that changed everything:

"The cancer is all gone."

Just twenty-eight days.

Four weeks.

But it felt like a lifetime lived in prayer, surrender, stillness, and supernatural strength.

I can still feel the moment.

I was sitting in the exam room, waiting for the doctor to come in. Waiting for news that could either steady me or shake me. My heart was quiet — more quiet than I expected. Not because I wasn't nervous, but because God had given me a peace that made no sense.

When the doctor walked in and said those words, my breath caught.

Tears filled my eyes instantly — not from fear this time, but from overwhelming gratitude.

Cancer-free.

Two words that wrapped themselves around my heart and squeezed out every ounce of tension I had been carrying. Two words that felt like God Himself whispering, *"I told you I was with you."*

I cried — but the tears weren't heavy.

They were holy.

Narrative Reflection

That moment marked me in a way I will never forget.

It wasn't just a medical victory — it was a spiritual one.

I thought about everything God had done leading up to this day:

- The whisper that told me to go to the mammogram
- The butterfly that showed up during my first biopsy
- The cardinal on the morning of my second surgery
- The believers God reconnected me with after decades
- The peace in the diagnosis room
- The protection over my children's hearts
- The timing of every appointment
- The prayers God answered before I prayed them
- The strength He gave when fear tried to rise
- The way He carried me through the quiet valleys

Every sign, every whisper, every reassurance had been pointing to this moment.

God had been weaving my healing long before I ever knew I needed it.

I realized something that day:

Healing is not just physical — healing is spiritual.

Healing changes:

- the way you see God
- the way you hear Him
- the way you trust Him

- the way you carry yourself
- the way you appreciate life
- the way you love
- the way you pray
- the way you speak

Healing rewires your faith.

I walked out of that exam room not just relieved — I walked out *renewed*.

Stronger. Softer. More aware of God's voice. More anchored in His promises.

God didn't just remove the cancer —

He removed fear.

He removed doubt.

He removed the parts of me that were surviving and restored the parts that were meant to be thriving.

What Day 28 Really Meant

Day 28 wasn't coincidence.

It was confirmation.

The number 28 represents "a complete cycle" in biblical symbolism — a God-orchestrated full circle moment.

In twenty-eight days:

- I met fear
- I met peace
- I met God in the quiet
- I met myself in the stillness
- I met healing in the valley
- And I met victory at the mountain

It was as if God said, *"I will not let this linger longer than necessary. This ends here."*

And it did.

I didn't just walk into healing — healing walked into me.

It shifted the atmosphere of my home.

It strengthened my marriage.

It impacted my children.

It softened my heart.

It deepened my relationship with God.

Day 28 became a memorial stone — a moment I will look back on for the rest of my life and say:

"This was God."

Miracles on the Operating Table

As I reflected on everything God had done, I began remembering all the predictions the doctors made — the things they warned me *might* happen, the possibilities they wanted to prepare me for. Their intentions were good, but their words were heavy.

And every time they spoke, I had one answer:

"It is well."

Not out of denial.

Not out of stubbornness.

But because my faith refused to surrender the peace God had given me.

Before surgery, they told me they might have to **take the nipple**.

It's the kind of news that shakes you — but I felt a stillness rise in me.

I whispered,

"It is well."

I trusted God with the part of me they were preparing to remove.

When I woke up from surgery, still groggy and disoriented, the surgeon came in and said:

"We didn't have to take it."

I exhaled the biggest breath.

Another miracle.

Before the second surgery, I was told,

"You will likely **lose sensation**."

Again I said,

"It is well."

I placed my trust in the God who created my body, not the predictions of man.

And on September 2, 2025—the day after Labor Day—I began radiation.

Exactly one year earlier, on September 3, 2024, the day after Labor Day, God had spoken words that changed everything:

"Leave. And don't come back."

I didn't know then that my obedience would prepare me for healing.

I didn't know that surrender would come before strength.

Radiation ended on September 8, 2025—eight days before September 16, my mother's birthday, and mine.

The same God who asked me to trust Him in the leaving met me again in the healing.

He does not waste obedience.

And He always finishes what He starts.

Scripture Meditations

- **Exodus 15:26** — "For I am the Lord that healeth thee."
- **Jeremiah 30:17** — "I will restore health unto thee…"
- **Psalm 103:2–3** — "Who healeth all thy diseases…"
- **Psalm 30:11** — "Thou hast turned my mourning into dancing…"

Reflection Questions

1. What is your "Day 28" — the moment God turned something around for you?
2. How has God shown Himself faithful in seasons that felt overwhelming?
3. What memorial markers has God placed in your life to remind you of His healing and protection?
4. How can you celebrate the victories God has given you — big or small?

Closing Prayer

Father, thank You for the miracle of healing. Thank You for carrying me through every moment of fear and flooding my heart with peace. Thank You for the victory You declared long before I ever saw it. Teach me to always remember Your faithfulness, to walk boldly in the healing You have given me, and to testify of Your goodness wherever I go. In Jesus' name, amen.

CHAPTER 21 — CLOSING REFLECTIONS

Opening Verse

"Faith is the substance of things hoped for, the evidence of things not seen."
– Hebrews 11:1

Journal Entry

As I reflect on the fullness of this journey — the whispers from God, the miracles in surgery, the unexpected reconnections, the healing, the tears, the valleys, and the victories — I see something I didn't see at the beginning:

God wasn't just healing my body.

He was transforming my life.

He was strengthening my spirit.

He was shifting my family.

He was breaking generational patterns.

He was rebuilding everything that loss tried to steal.

My walk of faith did not begin with cancer.

It began in **2022**, when I experienced loss after loss — seven losses in two years.

Grief after grief.

Valley after valley.

Wave after wave.

Yet even then, something in me clung tighter to God instead of pulling away.

I didn't hide.
I didn't curse God.
I didn't retreat.
I lifted my hands — even in heartbreak — and sang songs of worship.
I praised God through every storm.
Most people run from God during loss,
but I ran *toward* Him.
And little did I know...
my worship in 2022 and 2023, and my obedience in 2024, was preparing me for the battle of 2025.

A TRANSFORMED HUSBAND

One of the greatest miracles of this journey wasn't found on a scan —
it happened inside my home.
I watched my husband's faith transform before my eyes.
Danny prayed with a depth and tenderness I had never seen before.
His prayers were heartfelt... compassionate... powerful.
He wasn't repeating words — he was seeking God for *himself*.
When fear tried to rise in him, he didn't pull away from God —
he doubled down on his faith.
He told me one day, "Kim, the reason I can believe God through this is because of how I've watched you hold on to Him. I saw you lose so much — your parents, family members, people you loved — and you never let go of God. You praised Him anyway."
My obedience became his strength.
My worship became his blueprint.
My walk encouraged his own walk with God.
I didn't realize it then, but God was not just healing me —
He was healing us.
Strengthening our marriage.
Establishing our faith together.

Making our home a sanctuary of prayer.
This journey changed Danny's relationship with God —
not through sermons or church services,
but through watching God carry his wife.

GRIEF, GENERATIONS & JESUS

My mother never let me see her grieve.
Not once.
When her own mother died, she didn't cry in front of me.
She didn't show sadness.
She didn't show weakness.
She carried strength like a shield —
but her silence taught me something unintended:
"Don't show your children your tears.
Be strong.
Hide your pain."
So when my own storm hit, I tried to do the same.
I felt guilty for grieving.
Guilty for having weak moments.
Guilty for crying.
Until my children said,
"Mom, it's okay to cry. It's okay to let it out.
We're here."
That moment broke something in me —
and healed something at the same time.
My children gave me permission to grieve.
To feel.
To be human.
To lay down the cape of "strength" from the generation before me.
And then I remembered something profoundly healing:
Jesus wept.
Our Creator,
our Savior,
our Healer,

our King —
He wept.
If Jesus Himself made space for grief,
surely I could too.
This journal isn't about perfection.
It's about presence — the presence of God in every emotion,
every tear,
every valley,
every whisper,
every praise,
every moment I thought I was breaking.

PRACTICE DOESN'T MAKE PERFECT — PRACTICE MAKES PERMANENT

I used to think spiritual maturity was about doing things perfectly.

But this journey taught me something deeper:

Practice doesn't make perfect — practice makes permanent.

I practiced:

- trusting God
- praising God
- obeying God
- surrendering fear
- speaking Scripture over myself
- choosing gratitude
- listening for His whisper

And because I practiced it daily,
it became **permanent**.
Not because I was strong —
but because God was faithful.
This journey was not about flawless faith.
It was about *consistent* faith.

Faith that wavered but returned.
Faith that trembled but stayed.
Faith that questioned but obeyed.
Faith that cried but worshipped anyway.
Faith that God honored every step of the way.
Every time I grew weak, God whispered a verse.
Every time fear rose, God reminded me of a promise.
Every time my heart shook, God steadied me.
Gratitude pulled me out of fear.
Surrender pulled me out of doubt.
Scripture pulled me out of anxiety.
God pulled me out of everything.

LOOKING BACK — AND LOOKING FORWARD

When I look back, I don't just see cancer.
I see Christ.
I see:

- divine timing
- divine protection
- divine preparation
- divine people
- divine healing
- divine strength
- divine transformation
- divine completeness

I see a God who walked ahead of me, beside me, and behind me.
I see a God who allowed my husband to grow in his own faith through my testimony.
I see a God who allowed my children to break generational silence around grief.
I see a God who used every loss in 2022–2024 to prepare me for victory in 2025.
I see a God whose whispers were louder than my fear.
I see a God whose presence met me in every moment —

not because I was perfect,
but because He is.
This journey has taught me that faith is not a straight line —
it is a walk.
A daily choice.
A sacred rhythm of trust and surrender.
And through every step, God has been faithful.

Scripture Meditations

- **Psalm 27:13** — "I had fainted, unless I had believed to see the goodness of the Lord..."
- **2 Corinthians 12:9** — "My grace is sufficient..."
- **Romans 8:37** — "We are more than conquerors..."
- **Revelation 12:11** — "They overcame... by the word of their testimony..."

Reflection Questions

1. What parts of your life has God been quietly preparing long before you knew you'd need it?
2. How have your relationships or family been transformed in your valley seasons?
3. What generational patterns is God healing in you?
4. What does practicing faith look like in your daily life?

Closing Prayer

Lord, thank You for every loss You redeemed, every tear You caught, every moment You carried me, and every person You transformed through my journey. Strengthen my faith so that trust becomes permanent. Teach me to grieve honestly, worship consistently, and obey completely. Thank You for healing not only my body, but my family, my children, my marriage, and my heart. In Jesus' name, amen.

Chapter 22 — The Victory Bell 

(The Completion of the Journey)

Opening Verse

"This is the Lord's doing; it is marvellous in our eyes."
– Psalm 118:23

Journal Entry

September 8th.

A date that will forever be engraved in my heart.

It was the day I walked into MD Anderson Cancer Center for my **final** radiation treatment —

the fifth one God reduced from the twenty I was originally told I needed.

It was the day I would ring the radiation bell.

And even though I knew the bell was waiting for me,

I wasn't prepared for what that moment would do to my spirit.

I wasn't prepared for the emotions that would rise.

I wasn't prepared for the tears that would fall.

I wasn't prepared for the Holy Spirit that would fill the hallway.

I wasn't prepared for the weight of victory.

It became one of the most beautiful moments of my entire journey.

What We Wore Into Battle

That day, I wore a shirt that said:

"Be still and know."

The Scripture that had carried me through 2022,

through loss,

through diagnosis,

through surgery,

through treatment,

through fear,

through waiting,

through everything.

And Danny wore a shirt with Jesus standing on top of the devil saying:

"You mad bro?"

We didn't plan it.

We didn't coordinate it.

But it could not have been more prophetic.

My shirt declared **trust**.

His shirt declared **victory**.

Together, they declared the entire story:

Be still and know… because Jesus has already defeated every enemy.

The Walk to the Bell

When my fifth treatment ended, the nurse walked me toward the bell.

My heart began to beat differently — like it knew heaven was leaning in.

Staff began gathering.

Faces I had seen for weeks — faces full of compassion, dignity, and God's excellence.

My medical team — the ones God appointed for me before the foundation of the world — stepped forward with smiles that felt like sunlight.

They said:

"Today is your day."

And immediately, tears filled my eyes.

Danny's too.

We hadn't cried like this before.

We didn't even try to hold it back.

It felt like the presence of God wrapped around both of us in that hallway.

I could barely hold the rope.

I could barely breathe.

I could barely see through the tears.

But I felt God.

THE MEANING OF THE THREE RINGS

Before I rang the bell, the nurse said:

"Each ring means something."

The First Ring — VICTORY

She said:

"This one declares that the battle you endured has now come to an end."

As I pulled the rope the first time,

I felt the weight of every appointment,

every test,

every sleepless night,

every whisper,

every tear,

every miracle.

And I felt heaven echo:

Victory.

The Second Ring — STRENGTH

"This ring honors your strength," she said,

"and the strength it took to walk this journey."

As the bell sounded the second time,
I remembered the butterfly,
the cardinal,
the whispers from God,
Danny's prayers,
my children's faith,
my own hands lifted in worship even when I felt crushed.
This was **God's** strength in me.
Not mine.

The Third Ring — HOPE

"This final ring," she said,
"is for your future — and for the people who will come after you."
As the bell rang a third time,
I knew I wasn't just ringing for myself.
I was ringing for:

- every woman in that waiting room
- every mother
- every fighter
- every survivor
- every tear
- every valley
- every person who needed to know God still heals

I was ringing as a testimony.
I was ringing **hope**.

THE WOMEN IN THE WAITING ROOM

As I turned to walk out,
the women waiting for their treatment — women fighting their own battles —
began to **clap.**
They clapped like they were celebrating a sister.
They clapped like they felt my victory in their bones.

They clapped like they needed that hope too.
I turned to them, tears falling freely, and said:
"You're going to ring this bell too."
They nodded.
Some cried.
Some smiled through their pain.
Some put their hands over their hearts.
And at that moment,
I felt God whisper:
"This is why you fight — so they know it's possible."
Danny's Tears
Seeing Danny cry broke me open in a way nothing else had.
He held me tightly, overwhelmed by gratitude, joy, and reverence.
He said:
**"God healed you, Kim…
and He healed my faith too."**
I will never forget the sound of his voice.
I will never forget the way he held me.
I will never forget how proud he was — not just of me, but of God.
This journey changed him.
It deepened him.
It transformed him.
It made him a man who doesn't just believe **in** God —
but seeks to **hear God**.
The bell didn't just ring for my healing —
it rang for our marriage,
for our family,
for our spiritual legacy.

THE MOMENT I WILL NEVER FORGET

When the bell stopped echoing,
my heart whispered three words:
"It is finished."
Not the kind of finished that brings sadness —
but the kind that brings wholeness.

God took me through the fire
and brought me out without the smell of smoke.
The bell was not an ending —
it was an **exclamation mark**.
A punctuation of victory.
A sound of deliverance.
A shout of testimony.
A declaration of God's goodness.
A reminder that God completes what He begins.
It was the final note of a song heaven had been singing over
my life
from the beginning.
I will never forget that day.
It was —
and always will be —
one of the most beautiful
and holy
moments of my life.

Scripture Meditations

- **Psalm 118:23** — "This is the Lord's doing…"
- **Isaiah 58:8** — "Thy health shall spring forth speedily…"
- **Jeremiah 30:17** — "I will restore health unto thee…"
- **Psalm 103:2–3** — "Forget not all His benefits…"

Reflection Questions

1. What does your "victory bell" moment look like in your own life?
2. What battles has God carried you through that you can now celebrate?
3. Who needs to hear your testimony so they can find hope?

4. How has God used your journey to strengthen someone else's faith?

<u>Closing Prayer</u>

Lord, thank You for the sound of victory.
Thank You for the healing You completed,
the hope You restored,
the strength You renewed,
and the testimony You entrusted me with.
Let the echo of that bell
continue ringing in my spirit
all the days of my life.
May it remind me —
and everyone who reads this —
that You finish what You begin,
and You heal what others declare impossible.
In Jesus' name,
Amen.

AFTER THE STORY

Life After Healing

A Devotional Reflection

"O give thanks unto the Lord; for he is good: for his mercy endureth for ever."
— Psalm 107:1

Healing is not a moment.
Healing is a journey.
Healing is a life you grow into.

When the treatments end, when the appointments slow down, when the last bandage is removed, and when the radiation bell stops echoing in your spirit, something unexpected happens —

you begin to live again.

But you don't go back to who you were.

You can't.

You've seen too much.

You've felt too deeply.

You've been carried too faithfully.

There is a *before* healing and an *after* healing — and they are not the same.

A New Kind of Gratitude

After healing, gratitude becomes your natural posture.

Small moments take on a sacred weight:

the morning sun peeking through your window,

the sound of laughter in your home,

the simplicity of a quiet night,
even the ordinary chores that used to feel burdensome.
You begin to see beauty in places you once overlooked.
You wake up differently —
with a fresh awareness that *this day is a gift,*
this breath is a blessing,
this moment is holy.
Healing makes you more grateful,
more attentive,
more alive.

A New Way of Seeing God
Before the valley, you knew God.
But after the valley,
you *know* God.
You've seen His hand move in ways that defy explanation.
You've watched Him reveal what doctors could not.
You've felt Him calm storms inside you that medicine couldn't
touch.
You've witnessed His precision —
down to the **7th cut** on the biopsy,
down to the **5th radiation treatment**,
down to the exact people He assigned to your journey.
Life after healing means you see God everywhere —
in the details,
in the timing,
in the protection,
in the whispers,
in the restoration.
You no longer hope He is faithful —
you *know* He is.

A New Kind of Strength
Healing reveals a strength that is not your own.

It's a quiet strength, a steady strength — the kind that only comes through fire.

You realize:

- You are stronger than you believed.
- You are softer than you understood.
- You are braver than you imagined.
- You are wiser than before.
- You are more compassionate than ever.

But the most important realization?

Your strength was never your strength.

It was His.

He carried you.

He sustained you.

He fought for you.

He whispered to you.

He healed you.

Life after healing means you live from a place of divine strength rather than self-strength.

A New Capacity to Love

Pain softens.

Loss deepens.

Healing expands.

Your capacity to love your family grows because you saw their tears.

Your marriage strengthens because you fought as one.

Your patience grows because you learned how fragile life can be.

Your compassion grows because you know how much words matter.

Your love deepens because you understand the sacredness of time.

You don't take relationships for granted anymore.

You cherish differently.

You prioritize differently.
You listen differently.
You love differently.

A New Purpose
After the valley, purpose becomes clearer.
You realize:

- Your story is not yours to keep.
- Your healing is not just for you.
- Your testimony will become healing for someone else.
- Your "valley notes" will one day be someone's roadmap.
- Your strength will become someone's courage.
- Your faith will become someone's anchor.

You survived for a reason —
not to stay silent,
but to shine.
God didn't bring you out so you could move on.
He brought you out so you could move **others** forward.

A New Relationship With Peace
The peace that comes after healing is deeper than anything
you felt before.
It is a peace born from:

- surrender
- trust
- worship
- obedience
- brokenness
- rebuilding
- transformation

It is a peace that says:
**"If God brought me through that,
He will bring me through anything."**

It is a peace that stabilizes your mind.
It is a peace that softens your fears.
It is a peace that disarms anxiety.
It is a peace that guards your heart.
Life after healing means you live wrapped in the peace of God —
peace that only survivors understand.

Seeing Yourself Differently
Healing doesn't just change your perspective of God —
it changes your perspective of *you.*
You see strength where you once saw fragility.
You see courage where you once saw fear.
You see purpose where you once saw confusion.
You see clarity where you once saw uncertainty.
You see beauty where you once felt broken.
You walk taller,
speak softer,
love deeper,
worship louder,
and trust quicker.
Life after healing gives you a new identity —
a woman held, covered, strengthened, and delivered by God.

Healing Doesn't End the Journey — It Begins a New One
There is life after healing —
a full life,
a beautiful life,
a purposeful life,
a grateful life.
Life after healing is a **calling**
to live braver,
love deeper,
worship louder,
and testify boldly.

Your story did not end with cancer.
Your story is just beginning.
And now, on the other side of the valley,
your life becomes a living reminder that:
God heals.
God restores.
God redeems.
God finishes what He starts.

Scripture Meditations

- **Psalm 30:2** — "O Lord my God, I cried unto thee, and thou hast healed me."
- **Isaiah 58:8** — "Thy health shall spring forth speedily…"
- **Psalm 107:20** — "He sent His word, and healed them…"

Reflection Questions

1. What has healing taught you about God's character?
2. What areas of your life feel different after healing?
3. How is God calling you to use your testimony to encourage others?
4. What new purpose has emerged in your journey?

Closing Prayer

Lord, thank You for healing me and leading me into a new season full of purpose, strength, and joy.

Teach me to walk in my healing boldly and gratefully.

Let my life reflect Your goodness and become a testimony of Your faithfulness.

Use my story to encourage, uplift, and bring hope to others.
In Jesus' name, amen.

ᴘʀᴀɪsᴇ Fʀᴏᴍ ᴛʜᴇ Pᴇᴀᴋ

My Mountaintop After Healing

After everything God brought me through —
the losses, the diagnosis, the biopsies, the surgeries, the radiation, the waiting, the fear, the miracles, the whispers —

I wanted to thank Him from the highest place I could reach.

So I climbed **Clingman's Dome** again.

The highest point in the Smoky Mountains.

The same climb I promised myself I would never do again in 2021.

But this time... it was different.

This time, it was **personal**.

Every step up that mountain felt like a testimony.

Every breath reminded me that God had healed me.

Every glance at the sky reminded me how far He had carried me.

Every ache in my body reminded me of the strength He restored.

Every moment on that trail whispered:

"Look at what God has done."

As I walked, I wasn't just climbing a mountain —

I was climbing out of fear,

out of the valley,

out of loss,

out of uncertainty,

and into **another level of gratitude**.

When I reached the top, I lifted my hands in worship —

not because the climb was easy,

but because **He made it possible**.

I stood there with tears in my eyes

and praise in my heart,
breathing in the cool mountain air
and exhaling the weight of everything I had survived.
Up there, I felt the truth of Psalm 121 in my bones:
**"I will lift up mine eyes unto the hills,
from whence cometh my help.
My help cometh from the Lord."
— Psalm 121:1–2**
I thanked Him for healing me.
I thanked Him for protecting me.
I thanked Him for carrying me through every valley.
I thanked Him for restoring my strength.
I thanked Him for the life I still get to live.
I thanked Him because He is good —
not just on the mountaintop,
but in every step it took to get there.
Climbing Clingman's Dome became my physical declaration
of spiritual victory.
It was my way of saying:
**"I'm still here.
God kept me.
And I praise Him from the peak."**

 22 Life Lessons God Taught Me

Wisdom from the Valley, the Waiting, and the Victory

1. God prepares you long before the battle arrives.
Every loss in 2022–2024 strengthened my faith muscles for
the storm of 2025.
Nothing was wasted.
Nothing caught God off guard.

2. Obedience is the doorway to miracles.
My entire healing journey began with one act of obedience:
"Leave and don't come back."
Saying yes to God changed everything.

3. Worship is a weapon, not an accessory.
I didn't just sing — I fought.
Praise shifted atmospheres inside my home and inside my spirit.

**4. Fear doesn't leave instantly — it leaves gradually as
faith grows louder.**
I felt fear, but fear didn't hold me hostage.
Faith took up the louder seat.

5. Stillness is a spiritual strategy, not inactivity.
God taught me that being still is how you surrender control.
Stillness invites clarity.

Stillness invites peace.
Stillness invites God.

6. God speaks most clearly in quiet spaces.
His whisper met me in mornings, nights, prayers, tears, and
silence.
He never failed to answer.

7. Healing is a process, not a moment.
God healed my body through surgery,
my mind through Scripture,
my heart through worship,
and my home through unity.

8. Grief is not a lack of faith — grief is evidence of love.
Jesus wept.
So can we.
My children healed me by giving me permission to grieve out
loud.

9. God's compassion is woven into every detail.
From the butterfly to the cardinal,
from the right doctors to the right timing —
God compassionately orchestrated everything.

**10. Your testimony becomes someone else's survival
guide.**
I learned that what nearly broke me
will one day strengthen someone else.

11. God reveals what others overlook.
Test after test looked benign,
but God guided MD Anderson to the exact hidden place —
in the **7th** cut of **13**.
Seven — the number of completion.

12. Marriage strengthens in the fire when God is at the center.
Danny's faith deepened because of my walk.
My worship became his blueprint.
Our tears became our unity.
God healed both of us.

13. God assigns people to your journey.
A sorority sister from 30 years ago.
A classmate from 1989.
Two cancer survivors.
Two prayer warriors.
Two divine appointments.

14. The right medical team is a miracle in itself.
God assembled mine before the foundation of the world.
Their thoroughness saved my life.

15. God's timing is protective, not punishing.
If He delays, it's because He's aligning.
If He pauses, it's because He's preparing.
If He closes a door, it's because danger was behind it.

16. Peace is not the absence of problems — it's the presence of God.
Peace covered me in doctor's rooms,
during biopsies,
in hallways,
and even on tables.

17. Joy is an act of resistance.
Smiling on diagnosis day wasn't denial.
It was the Holy Spirit rising in me.

18. Faith is a daily choice, not a one-time declaration.
Every day, I chose trust.
Every day, I chose worship.
Every day, I chose surrender.

19. Every battle contains a blessing.
Cancer broke things in me that needed breaking —
and rebuilt things I didn't know were missing.

20. God finishes what He begins — every time.
From the first whisper
to the last radiation bell,
God completed the work.

21. Victory must be celebrated.
I didn't expect the emotion of ringing that bell.
But heaven celebrated with me.
And the women waiting in the next room clapped for their own
future victory.

22. Faith over fear isn't a phrase — it's a lifestyle.
It's the way I choose to live.
It's the way I pray.
It's the way I worship.
It's the way God carried me.
It is my testimony.

❧ My Healing Rituals & Daily ❧ Practices

How I Stayed Anchored, Calm, and Connected to God During My Journey

Healing is not just medical — it is spiritual, emotional, mental, and physical.

During my journey, I discovered that healing is something you walk out **daily**, not something that happens all at once.

Here are the practices and rituals that carried me, grounded me, and surrounded me with God's presence through my valley.

1. Morning Stillness

Before the world woke up, I sat in silence.

No music.

No phone.

Just God.

I would breathe slowly, let my heart settle, and whisper, "Lord, I'm here."

That stillness — even for 5–10 minutes — changed everything.

It quieted fear before fear could rise.

It re-centered my spirit.

It reminded me that peace is possible in every season.

2. Scripture on Repeat

I didn't read to finish — I read to **breathe**.

Some Scriptures stayed with me for months:

- "Be still and know…"

- "The Lord will fight for you..."
- "Fear not, for I am with you..."

When my thoughts started racing, I replaced fear with Scripture.
It was spiritual medicine.
A daily dose of truth.

3. Worship as Atmosphere

I played worship constantly — in the morning, while getting ready, in the car, in moments of anxiety, in the shower, before appointments.
Worship wasn't background noise.
It was atmosphere-shifting.
It turned my home into sanctuary space.
It flooded my mind with reminders of who God is.

4. Walking Outside

Fresh air became part of my healing.
Some days I walked slowly.
Some days I didn't walk far.
But every step reminded me:
"I'm still here. God is still carrying me."
Nature became a daily sermon —
a reminder that God creates new life again and again.

5. Gratitude Lists

Even before I felt grateful,
I wrote down three things a day:
- Something God did
- Something I learned
- Something I loved

Some days the list was long.
Some days the list was short.
But gratitude was a spiritual discipline that changed my perspective.

6. Limiting Noise & Negativity

I became intentional about what I allowed near my spirit.
Some conversations didn't get access.
Some voices stayed at a distance.
Some people meant well but brought fear, not faith.
Protecting my peace was part of my healing.

7. Prayer Walks in My House

Sometimes I walked room to room praying softly:
"Lord, fill this home with peace."
"Protect my family."
"Cover this atmosphere."
My home became a place of worship.
Prayer became a rhythm, not an event.

8. Speaking Life Over My Body

I spoke to my body like it was loved —
because God created it.
I said things like:
"You are healing."
"You are strong."
"You will recover."
"God is restoring you."
Words matter.
And my body responded to truth spoken with faith.

9. Rest Without Guilt

Rest was part of my obedience.
Part of my trust.
Part of my healing.
I stopped apologizing for needing downtime.
I stopped feeling guilty for naps.
I stopped pushing myself to be "productive."
Rest is holy.

10. Ending My Day in God's Peace
At night, I listened to soft worship or Scripture audio until I
fell asleep.
If anxiety whispered, I whispered back:
"Lord, be with me."
And He was.
Every night.

Final Reflection
My healing rituals weren't routines —
they were **lifelines.**
They carried me.
They grounded me.
They kept me close to God when fear tried to distance me.
They helped me hear His whisper when the world was loud.
These practices didn't just help me survive —
they helped me heal *whole.*
They transformed me.
And they can carry you too.

 # TEN PRAYERS FOR THE JOURNEY

These prayers were born out of real moments —
real tears,
real fear,
real surrender,
real miracles,
and a very real God who carried me.
May they carry you too.

1. A Prayer for When Fear Tries to Rise

Father, in the moments when fear tries to overtake my mind, steady me. Remind me who You are — my refuge, my fortress, my healer, my defender, my peace. Silence the racing thoughts and quiet the anxious places inside of me. Let Your presence wrap around me like a warm blanket and push out every trace of fear. Teach me to breathe deeply, slowly, intentionally, knowing that every breath is held in Your hands. Remind me that fear is not from You — peace is. Strength is. Courage is. Love is. I renounce fear in the name of Jesus and choose to trust You right here, right now. Amen.

2. A Prayer for Waiting on Test Results

Lord, I place every test, scan, image, number, and result into Your capable hands. The waiting is hard. My thoughts try to run ahead of You. My emotions feel fragile. But I know You are already in the waiting room, already in the results, al-

ready in tomorrow. Help me rest in Your sovereignty. Calm my mind, guard my heart, and let Your peace fill every space where fear tries to sneak in. I trust that whatever is revealed is something You already knew — and something You will carry me through. Amen.

3. A Prayer Before Surgery or Procedures

God, as I lie down to be examined, scanned, biopsied, or operated on, I ask for Your presence to fill the room. Guide the hands of every surgeon, nurse, anesthesiologist, and technician. Let wisdom flow through them. Let accuracy guide them. Let peace surround them. Protect my body from harm and lead my medical team to exactly what needs to be seen, removed, treated, or healed. Overshadow the entire procedure with Your glory. I surrender this moment to You fully, knowing that You never leave me, not even here. Amen.

4. A Prayer for Strength on Hard Days

Father, sometimes my strength feels thin. Sometimes I feel tired in my soul, not just my body. I ask for Your supernatural strength to rise in me. Strength that doesn't come from willpower, but from Your Spirit. Strength that doesn't crumble under pressure. Strength that holds me when I feel like falling apart. Teach me to lean into You instead of trying to carry everything myself. Let Your power be made perfect in my weakness today and every day. Amen.

5. A Prayer for Peace in the Middle of the Night

Lord, when the night feels long and quiet, and the world feels still, my thoughts often grow louder. I ask for Your peace to descend upon me like gentle rain. Calm the anxiety that threatens rest. Quiet the "what ifs." Fill my bedroom with Your presence — let angels stand guard around my home. Allow me to sleep deeply, safely, and peacefully. Let my dreams be filled with Your voice, Your love, Your reassurance. Remind me that even in the dark, You are light. Amen.

6. A Prayer for Comfort in Grief

God, You know my heartbreak. You see the places where sorrow still touches me, shaped by years of loss. Wrap Your arms around me and comfort me the way only You can. Remind me that grief is not weakness but evidence of love. Teach me to grieve honestly and freely. Heal the parts of me that feel bruised by memories. Turn my mourning into joy in Your perfect timing. Walk with me through every wave of sadness until peace fills the empty spaces again. Amen.

7. A Prayer for Family and Loved Ones

Lord, thank You for the people who walk with me — for my husband, my children, my friends, and my family. Bless them for every prayer they prayed, every tear they shed, every moment they stood beside me. Strengthen their hearts. Protect their minds. Deepen their faith. Let our home be a sanctuary filled with peace, love, compassion, and unity. Cover Danny as he leads and supports me. Cover Zachary and Madison as they continue growing into their own walks with You. Bind us together, and let our family be a testimony of Your goodness. Amen.

8. A Prayer for Discernment and Guidance

Heavenly Father, guide my steps, my decisions, and my thoughts. Lead me in clarity, not confusion. Help me discern Your voice above all others. If something is not from You, let it fall away quickly. If something is from You, confirm it with peace. Give me the wisdom to make choices that align with Your will. Direct my heart into every door You open — and away from every door You close. I trust Your leadership in every part of this journey. Amen.

9. A Prayer for Healing and Restoration

Lord, thank You for healing my body and restoring my health. Continue to renew every cell, every organ, every hormone, every system. Restore what treatments affected. Strengthen my immune system. Renew my energy. Rebalance my emotions. Restore my joy, my peace, my sleep, my appetite, my strength. Let Your healing flow from the inside out. And Lord, heal not just my body — but my heart, my memories, my fears, and my faith. Amen.

10. A Prayer for Hope for the Future

Father, thank You that my story doesn't end with diagnosis — it continues with destiny. Fill me with hope for the future. Give me dreams again. Give me vision again. Give me purpose again. Help me walk boldly in the calling You created me for. I declare that my future is bright, blessed, protected, and guided by You. Let my life be a testimony of faith, courage, and victory. In Jesus' name, amen.

22 Faith Declarations

Speaking Life Over Your Journey

Speak these out loud.

Declare them over your life, your mind, your body, and your future.

There is power in your words — and victory in your voice.

1. I declare that fear has no authority over my life.
God has not given me the spirit of fear, and fear cannot rule where God dwells.

2. I declare that God goes before me in every situation.
Nothing surprises Him; He prepares every detail in advance.

3. I declare that God is healing every part of me — body, mind, and spirit.
His restoration is complete and continuous.

4. I declare that I am surrounded by God's presence and protected by His peace.
His peace guards my heart and mind in Christ Jesus.

5. I declare that God's voice is louder than any negative report or fearful thought.
I hear His whisper clearly and confidently.

6. I declare that God's timing in my life is perfect.
He is never late, and He never misses.

7. I declare that I am stronger than every battle I face because the Lord is my strength.
My weakness is the doorway to His power.

8. I declare that God's plans for me are good, hopeful, and full of purpose.
My future is secure in Him.

9. I declare that no weapon formed against me will prosper.
Every attack is defeated in Jesus' name.

10. I declare that God is working all things together for my good.
Even what the enemy meant for harm, God is turning into testimony.

11. I declare that I am not alone — God is with me, beside me, and within me.
His nearness is my comfort.

12. I declare that I am loved deeply, wholly, completely by God.
Nothing can separate me from His love.

13. I declare that my home is covered in peace, unity, and divine protection.
The atmosphere of my home shifts in God's presence.

14. I declare that healing flows through my body daily.
Every system, cell, tissue, and hormone aligns with God's design.

15. I declare that joy will rise in me each morning.
Joy is not a feeling — it is a gift from God.

16. I declare that my mind is sound, stable, and anchored in truth.
I reject confusion and embrace clarity from the Holy Spirit.

17. I declare that I hear God's voice clearly.
He guides me, instructs me, and leads me with peace.

18. I declare that I walk in bold faith and unshakeable confidence.
My faith is stronger than my fear.

19. I declare that God will use my story to inspire and heal others.
My testimony is a tool for His glory.

20. I declare that what God starts, He finishes.
He is the Author and Finisher of my faith.

21. I declare that every battle I face becomes a place of victory.
I do not fight for victory — I fight **from** victory.

****22. I declare that my life will forever proclaim:**
"God is faithful. God is good. God is my healer."**
This is my testimony.
This is my declaration.
This is my truth — forever.

22 REFLECTIONS OF FAITH OVER FEAR

Lessons God Taught Me in the Valley

1. God's whisper is stronger than fear's shout.
Fear is loud and immediate, but God's whisper is steady, consistent, and trustworthy. I learned to lean in and listen closely.

2. Obedience opens doors fear tries to close.
My entire story changed because I obeyed God's voice — even when I didn't understand it.

3. Worship is warfare.
Every lifted hand, every whispered song, every tearful praise pushed back the darkness and made room for God's presence.

4. God prepares you long before He reveals the battle.
My losses in 2022–2024 were devastating, but they strengthened my spiritual muscles for the battle of 2025.

5. Miracles often unfold slowly, detail by detail.
It wasn't one miracle — it was dozens, stitched together by God's hand.

6. Stillness is not inactivity — it is strategy.
When God said, *"Be still,"* He wasn't telling me to stop; He was telling me to trust.

7. Strength is found in surrender, not striving.
The more I released control, the more God strengthened me
for the journey.

**8. God places the right people in your life at the right
time.**
A sorority sister from 30 years ago.
A classmate from Alabama I hadn't seen since 1989.
All divinely timed.

9. Your testimony is someone else's survival guide.
God does not waste pain. Someone needs what you survived.

10. Grief is not weakness — it is testimony.
Even Jesus wept. My grief didn't disqualify me; it made room
for God's comfort.

11. Love makes room for honesty.
My children gave me permission to grieve publicly — something
my mother never modeled. Their love healed me.

**12. God heals in layers — body, mind, spirit, relation-
ships.**
This journey healed my marriage, restored communication,
and deepened my faith.

13. Prayer is not a last resort — it's the lifeline.
Danny's prayers carried me. My own prayers steadied me. God's
answer strengthened me.

14. God's timing is perfect, even when it feels painful.
Seven losses.
Seventh cut.
Seven — the number of completion.
Nothing in my story was random.

15. God reveals what others overlook.
Test after test looked benign — but God guided MD Anderson to the exact place where the cancer hid.

16. Victory is not the absence of fear — it's choosing faith anyway.
I felt fear — but fear didn't get to sit on the throne of my heart.

17. Faith grows when you stop asking "why" and start trusting "Who."
I stopped needing explanations and leaned into His character instead.

18. God heals the parts of you you never knew were broken.
This journey healed childhood patterns, grief patterns, and generational silence.

19. Joy is holy resistance.
Smiling on diagnosis day wasn't delusion — it was the Holy Spirit rising within me.

20. God's presence makes even hospital rooms holy ground.
I felt Him in the waiting, in the recovery room, in the hallways, in the quiet — everywhere.

21. God's faithfulness becomes clearer in hindsight.
When I look back, I don't just see cancer.
I see Christ.

22. Faith over fear is a daily decision — not a one-time moment.
I didn't get through this because I was strong.
I got through this because God was.
Every day, in every moment, I chose Him.

A Letter to My Mother 

Momma,
I never imagined I would walk through a battle like this without you here. There were so many moments when I longed to hear your voice, your wisdom, your laughter, your prayers. But even though you were not physically with me, your spirit never left my side.

There were nights when fear tried to rise, and I could almost hear you say,

"Baby, God's got you."

And He did.

You taught me how to trust Him.

How to pray.

How to walk in faith even when I didn't understand.

How to place everything in His hands and stand still until He moved.

Your faith didn't just shape me — it carried me.

I remembered you when the waiting was long.

When the diagnosis shook me.

When the doctors were unsure.

When I needed to be strong for my children.

When grief resurfaced during moments I thought I had already healed.

You never let me see you grieve your own mother, and for years I thought that strength meant silence. But through this journey, I learned something you never had the chance to teach me:

Strength isn't hiding. Strength is holding on to God while you cry.

Strength is letting grief breathe.
Strength is showing your children honesty and still letting them
see you worship.
Momma, your death taught me to live differently.
Your faith taught me how to trust God in impossible moments.
Your resilience taught me how to press through when everything felt heavy.
And during this journey, I felt you everywhere —
in the Scriptures that carried me,
in the songs that comforted me,
in the butterfly that appeared before my biopsy,
in the strength that rose in me when I didn't know how to stand,
in the warmth that settled over me when I was afraid.
I felt you in the way I comforted my children through their fear —
the same way you comforted me.
And when I rang the radiation bell, Momma...
I imagined you smiling — the way you always smiled when I
overcame something hard.
Your memory strengthened me.
Your legacy empowered me.
Your love surrounded me.
And this book — this journey — this testimony — is part of
your legacy too.
Thank you for planting faith inside of me.
Thank you for teaching me who God is.
Thank you for every prayer you whispered over my life.
I carried those prayers into the valley —
and I carried them out with victory.
Momma... thank you for sharing your birthday with me.
Thank you for sharing your life with me.
And even now,
we're still sharing — forever connected — 9.16.
I miss you, Momma.
But I honor you with every breath of this testimony.
Your little red girl,
Kimmie

❧ WORSHIP PLAYLIST: WORSHIP ❧ THROUGH THE VALLEY

Songs That Carried Me When Words Failed

There were moments in this journey when I had no words left to pray — moments when fear was louder than my thoughts, when grief felt heavy, when silence felt sacred yet overwhelming.

In those moments, **God used worship to breathe life back into me.**

Worship became my oxygen.

Worship became my refuge.

Worship became my spiritual weapon.

Worship became the bridge between fear and faith.

These are the **22 songs** that carried me through the storm — songs that strengthened me, steadied me, and reminded me that God was always near.

May they carry you too.

1. My Fear Doesn't Stand a Chance (Stand in Your Love)
This song broke fear off of me again and again.

Every time anxiety tried to rise, this song reminded me that fear cannot grow where God's love is present.

The lyrics feel like a shield — "My fear doesn't stand a chance when I stand in Your love."

It wasn't just a song; it was spiritual **warfare.**

A declaration.

A boundary line drawn in the Spirit.

Fear had to bow.

Reflection:
This song taught me that fear isn't an identity I carry — love is.

2. This Is Amazing Grace — Phil Wickham

This song made me lift my hands in gratitude even on my hardest days.
It reminded me that everything God did — every miracle, every protection, every whisper — flowed from His **amazing grace**.
There were mornings I played this just to remind my heart:
"He breaks the power of sin and darkness — His love is mighty and so much stronger."
The grace that saved my soul was the same grace that carried me through cancer.
Reflection:
Grace didn't just save me — grace sustained me.

3. Made for More — Josh Baldwin

In the valley, it's easy to feel small, lost, or afraid.
This song reminded me that I was made for more —
more purpose,
more strength,
more courage,
more life.
It pulled my focus away from the diagnosis and back onto destiny.
Hearing "You're not done with me yet" breathed life into me.
Reflection:
This song reminded me that my calling didn't disappear in the storm — it was strengthened by it.

4. Don't Fight Alone — Jon Reddick

There were days when this journey felt heavy, and I wondered if anyone truly understood.
This song reminded me that God never meant for us to fight our battles in isolation.
It made me think of my husband's prayers,

my children's love,
my church's support,
my friends' encouragement,
and God's presence beside me in every room.
Reflection:
This song told me: "You are surrounded — not alone."

5. Battle Belongs — Phil Wickham

This became one of my most powerful declarations.
Every time fear tried to take control, this song reminded me:
"The battle belongs to the Lord."
Not the doctors.
Not the diagnosis.
Not fear.
Not the unknown.
God.
It shifted the weight from my shoulders onto His.
Reflection:
Surrender isn't weakness — it's strength wrapped in trust.

6. The Well — Casting Crowns

When I felt spiritually tired or emotionally drained, this song
drew me back to the Source.
I learned that I didn't have to pour from empty places — I could
drink deeply from God's presence.
It became a reminder:
"Leave it all behind and come to the well."
Reflection:
God is the well that never runs dry — the water that always
restores.

7. Be Still and Know — CeCe Winans

This song echoed the Scripture that carried me — Psalm 46:10.
CeCe's voice wrapped around my spirit like a blanket, whispering
peace into places that felt shaken.

It helped me understand that *stillness* isn't passive — it's holy.

It's trust.

It's surrender.

Reflection:

This song taught me that stillness is where God does His deepest work.

8. I Trust in God — Elevation Worship

This song became my daily anthem.

Through biopsies, waiting rooms, surgeries, and radiation — I trusted God.

This song helped me speak that trust out loud.

Every line felt like a declaration over my life:

"I trust in God — my Savior."

Reflection:

Trust is a choice, and this song helped me choose it daily.

9. Be Still and Know — Steven Curtis Chapman

This was the version that helped me slow down my racing mind.

When anxiety wanted to take over, this song reminded me that God was already handling what I could not.

Reflection:

Stillness refocused my heart on the One who was in control.

10. Goodness of God — CeCe Winans

I cried through this song more than any other.

Because even through loss, grief, fear, and diagnosis — God had been good to me.

Not because of circumstances, but because of His nature.

"I have lived in the goodness of God" became a line I held close.

Reflection:

This song reminded me to look at my life through the lens of God's goodness, not my pain.

11. Oceans — Hillsong UNITED

This song taught me how to walk by faith when I didn't understand the path.

My diagnosis became my ocean,

my unknown waters,

my place where feet could fail.

But God didn't let me sink.

Reflection:

God calls us deeper not to drown us — but to meet us there.

12. Promises — Maverick City Music

Every promise of God stood firm when my emotions did not.

This song became my anchor during long waits and uncertain

moments.

"He's faithful through generations"

hit different when I remembered my parents' faith and legacy.

Reflection:

God's promises don't expire — they endure.

13. Way Maker — Sinach

This song reminded me of what God was doing behind the

scenes.

Even when I didn't see movement,

God was making a way.

Even when I didn't feel Him,

He was working.

Reflection:

My story is proof that God makes a way where there is none.

14. Jireh — Elevation Worship & Maverick City Music

This song reminded me that God is enough —

emotionally,

spiritually,

physically,

financially.

He is my Provider in every way.

Reflection:
Provision is more than financial — God provides peace, strength, and presence too.

15. It Is Well — Bethel Music (Kristene DiMarco)
Singing "It is well" during storms doesn't mean everything is okay —
it means **your soul is anchored** even when life is not.
This song pulled me back into peace again and again.
Reflection:
Peace isn't the absence of waves — it's the presence of Christ.

16. Surrounded (This Is How I Fight My Battles)
This song taught me that worship is spiritual warfare.
Lifting my hands, even with tears in my eyes, became my victory stance.
Reflection:
I was surrounded by God, even when I felt surrounded by fear.

17. You Know My Name — Tasha Cobbs Leonard
There were moments I felt unseen or overwhelmed.
This song reminded me that God knew every detail of my journey —
every tear,
every fear,
every moment.
Reflection:
I never walked through a single moment unnoticed.

18. Refiner — Maverick City Music
This song taught me that refinement isn't punishment — it's preparation.
The fire didn't burn me — it purified me.
It shaped me.
Reflection:
God used the valley to refine me, not to destroy me.

19. The Blessing — Kari Jobe & Elevation Worship
This song covered my home, my children, my family, and my future.
Every time I played it, peace filled my home like a warm, quiet presence.
Reflection:
God's blessing reaches generations — past, present, and future.

20. Never Lost — CeCe Winans
Jesus has never lost a battle —
and my story wasn't going to be His first.
This song strengthened me when fear tried to rewrite the narrative.
Reflection:
Victory is in God's nature — and He shared that victory with me.

21. Precious Lord, Take My Hand — Luther Barnes
My mother's favorite song.
Hearing it made me feel her presence and her faith beside me.
This was the song she would have whispered over me during every part of my journey.
Reflection:
This song connected me to my mother's love, faith, and legacy.

22. Eye of the Storm — Ryan Stevenson
This song became a reminder that even in life's hardest seasons,
Jesus stands at the center holding everything together.
When the wind blew
and the waves rose
and the diagnosis tried to shake me —
He stayed.
Reflection:
The storm did not define me — God's presence did.

How to Use This Playlist

- Play these songs during quiet moments
- Sing them during prayer or journaling
- Use them to replace anxious thoughts with worship
- Let them fill your home with peace
- Worship however God leads you — lift your hands, sit still, cry, rejoice

Worship carried me through the valley.
May it carry you too.

A Word Before You Continue

Before you turn the page and continue deeper into this devotional journey, I want to pause with you for a moment.

You've walked with me through the valleys, the victories, the stillness, the worship, the miracles, and the healing. You've read the reflections, prayed the prayers, and perhaps felt your own emotions rising in the process.

This is a sacred point in the journey —

a place to breathe,

to settle your heart,

to let the Holy Spirit minister to you

before you step into the Scriptures that carried me.

The next pages are written **for you** —

a prayer spoken over your life,

questions God asked me that may now speak deeply to you,

and reflections that invite you to hear God's whisper in your own story.

My hope is that as you enter this section, you will begin to experience God not only as the God who healed me, but as the God who sees *you*.

The God who walks with *you*.

The God who comforts *you*.

The God who strengthens *you*.

The God who loves *you*.

Take a breath.

Slow down.

Let your heart soften.

Let your spirit open.

And now, as you turn the page, may you feel God drawing close — ready to speak, ready to comfort, ready to guide, and ready to meet you exactly where you are.

 # A PRAYER FOR THE WOMAN READING THIS BOOK

Dear Sister, if your eyes are on this page right now, I believe God orchestrated this moment.

Not by accident.

Not by coincidence.

Not by chance.

God knows exactly what you're carrying.

He knows the fears you don't say out loud.

He knows the prayers you whisper in the dark.

He knows the questions you're afraid to ask.

He knows the weight that sits quietly on your chest at night.

And right now, I want to pray for you — not as an author, but as a sister who has walked through the valley and seen the faithfulness of God.

Father, I lift up this precious woman to You.
You know her name.
You know her story.
You know her tears.
You know her strength and You know her breaking points.
Wrap Your arms around her
and let her feel the nearness of Your presence.
Let Your peace settle over her like warm oil.
Quiet the storms in her mind.
Silence every lie of fear.
Speak truth to the deepest parts of her soul.

Let her know that she is not walking alone —
that You are with her in the valley,
with her in the waiting,
with her in the questions,
with her in the unknown.
Give her courage to trust You in every season.
Give her strength to keep walking.
Give her clarity where confusion has lived.
Give her hope where disappointment has settled.
Give her joy where heaviness has lingered.
Give her rest where exhaustion has taken root.
Lord, remind her that Your plans for her are still good.
Remind her that Your timing is still perfect.
Remind her that Your love has not changed.
Remind her that miracles still happen —
and that she is not forgotten.
Let her feel Your healing power in her body.
Let her feel Your comfort in her heart.
Let her feel Your presence in her home.
Let her feel Your guidance in her decisions.
And Father, if she is in a valley, lead her through it.
If she is in a storm, speak "Peace, be still."
If she is afraid, whisper "Fear not, for I am with you."
Hold her close.
Carry her gently.
Strengthen her daily.
*And remind her that **faith over fear is possible***
because You are faithful.
In Jesus' name,
Amen.

QUESTIONS GOD ASKED ME — AND QUESTIONS FOR YOUR JOURNEY

As I walked through the hardest season of my life, God asked me questions that reshaped my faith, my identity, and my healing.

These same questions may become turning points in your journey, too.

Spend time with each one.

Write your answers slowly.

Let God speak to your heart through them.

1. "Do you trust Me?"

Really trust Me — with the unknown, the timing, the outcome, the process?

Reflect:

Where is God asking me to trust Him deeper?

2. "Will you surrender what you are trying to control?"

Healing happens when control is released.

Reflect:

What am I still gripping tightly that God is asking me to surrender?

3. "Will you let Me speak in the stillness?"

God speaks in whispers, not noise.

Reflect:

Where can I create more stillness in my life?

4. "Will you believe that I am good, even here?"
Even in fear.
Even in loss.
Even in waiting.
Reflect:
How have I seen God's goodness in my valley?

5. "Who do you say I am in this season?"
Your view of God becomes your anchor.
Reflect:
Who is God to me right now — Healer, Protector, Comforter,
Provider, Father?

6. "Will you let Me heal more than your body?"
He wants to heal your mind, your emotions, your memories.
Reflect:
What part of my life needs healing that I haven't talked about?

7. "Will you worship while you wait?"
Worship breaks chains that fear tries to forge.
Reflect:
What happens in my heart when I worship?

8. "Will you walk with Me into the next chapter?"
The valley was not the end — it was preparation.
Reflect:
What is God calling me into next?

Wʜᴀᴛ I Kɴᴏᴡ Nᴏᴡ

A Devotional Epilogue

There are some things in life you can only learn by walking through valleys.

Some wisdom you can only gain through tears.

Some truths you can only understand when God carries you through something you never imagined you'd survive.

Looking back now — at the fear, the pain, the grief, the surgeries, the radiation, the miracles, the whispers, the signs, the worship, the stillness, the divine timing — I see God with a clarity I never had before.

This is what I know now.

1. I know now that God was preparing me long before the battle began.

Every loss from 2022 to 2024 felt like a breaking, but it was really a building.

He strengthened me quietly, piece by piece, so I would not collapse in 2025.

I didn't walk into this storm empty —

I walked in equipped.

2. I know now that the whisper of God is more powerful than the shout of fear.

His whisper — *"Leave and don't come back"* —

began a journey that saved my life.

His whisper guided every appointment,

every decision,

every moment when fear tried to return.

3. I know now that stillness is a spiritual strategy.
"Be still and know" is not passive.
It is surrender.
It is trust.
It is warfare.
It is how you anchor your soul when the ground is shaking.
Stillness saved my sanity.
Stillness restored my peace.
Stillness became the place where God rebuilt me.

4. I know now that God places people in your life on purpose, not by accident.
A sorority sister from thirty years ago.
A classmate from Alabama I hadn't seen since 1989.
My medical team at MD Anderson.
Every nurse, every technician, every doctor.
My husband.
My children.
My prayer warriors.
Not one person in my story was random.
God handpicked every one.

5. I know now that worship changes everything.
Worship was my oxygen.
Worship was my refuge.
Worship was my warfare.
Worship was how I kept breathing.
Worship was how I survived.
I lifted my hands when I was strong —
and I lifted them when I was broken.
And God met me every single time.

6. I know now that my tears were not a sign of weakness — they were a sign of surrender.
I learned to grieve honestly, not silently.

To cry, not hide.
To feel, not pretend.
Jesus wept.
So can we.
And my children healed me by giving me permission to grieve
out loud.

7. I know now that God heals in layers.
He healed my body through surgery.
He healed my heart through worship.
He healed my mind through Scripture.
He healed my marriage through unity.
He healed generational patterns through truth.
Healing wasn't just physical — it was total.

8. I know now that God leads with compassion.
From the butterfly to the cardinal...
From the 7th cut to the 5th treatment...
From the divine timing to the smallest comforts...
God's compassion was woven into every detail.

9. I know now that the valley reveals what the mountaintop cannot.
I found God in the diagnosis room.
I found Him on the biopsy table.
I found Him in the quiet nights.
I found Him in the waiting.
I found Him in the tears.
The valley didn't hide God —
it revealed Him.

10. I know now that victory must be celebrated.
I didn't expect to cry when I rang the bell.
But heaven celebrated with me.
My husband cried beside me.

My medical team clapped.
The women waiting applauded.
I told them, "You will ring the bell too."
And I meant it.
That moment was an exclamation mark
on a story only God could have written.

11. I know now that faith over fear isn't a slogan — it's a lifestyle.
It's choosing trust when fear feels easier.
It's choosing worship when worry feels louder.
It's choosing stillness when panic wants to rise.
It's choosing to believe that:
"God is here.
God is working.
God is faithful.
And God will finish what He started."

12. I know now that God wrote every chapter of my healing long before I lived it.
He prepared the team.
He prepared the hands.
He prepared the timing.
He prepared the path.
He prepared my heart.
He prepared my faith.
Nothing was accidental.
Everything was aligned.

13. I know now that I am not who I was — I am stronger.
Stronger in faith.
Stronger in hope.
Stronger in worship.

Stronger in spirit.
Stronger in purpose.
And every valley, every tear, every prayer, every miracle contributed to that strength.

14. I know now that this story will outlive me.
My healing is not just for me —
it will comfort someone else.
It will encourage another woman.
It will lift someone who feels afraid.
It will shine a light for someone walking through their own valley.
My testimony is my assignment.

Closing Reflection
This is what I know now:
God is good.
God is faithful.
God is healer.
God is protector.
God is provider.
God is comforter.
God is whisperer.
God is present.
God is sovereign.
God is kind.
And through every moment of this journey —
from diagnosis to healing,
from fear to faith,
from tears to testimony —
I know now more than ever that my life is in His hands.

# REFLECTION PAGES

A Guided Journal for Your Healing Journey

1. Reflection: Where God Met Me in the Valley

Every valley has holy moments — whispers, signs, small mercies, unexpected comforts. In the middle of fear, God often meets us quietly: in a sunrise, in a verse, in a dream, in the gentleness of someone's words, or in the silence of our own thoughts. Reflecting on where God met you helps you see the full tapestry of His presence.

Journal Prompts:

- Where did I see God's hand in my hardest moments?
- What were the subtle whispers or signs He gave me?
- What comfort did He provide that only God could have given?

2. Reflection: Moments of Fear, Moments of Faith

Fear and faith often stand side by side. Your fear does not disqualify your faith — it reveals your humanity. Your faith reveals God's strength. Looking back helps you see not just what scared you, but how far God carried you.

Journal Prompts:

- What moments of fear stand out most?
- How did God steady me in those exact moments?
- What Scriptures helped me push fear back?

3. Reflection: Worship as Warfare

You lived this. Worship became your oxygen. It was how you fought when your strength wavered. Writing your worship story helps you remember how powerful worship truly is.

Journal Prompts:

- What worship moments strengthened me?
- What songs carried me through the storm?
- How did worship shift my emotions or my atmosphere?

4. Reflection: Healing Beyond the Body

Healing is rarely just physical. God heals emotional wounds, buried grief, generational silence, anxiety, and broken trust. Take a moment to reflect on the layers God healed in you.

Journal Prompts:

- What emotional wounds did God reveal during my journey?
- Where do I feel lighter now than before?
- What parts of my heart did God restore?

5. Reflection: The People God Assigned to Me

Your sorority sister.
Your high school friend.
Your team at MD Anderson.
Your husband.
Your children.
These were not random people — they were divine assignments.

Journal Prompts:

- Who did God send to walk with me?
- What impact did their words or presence have?
- How did God use other people to strengthen my faith?

6. Reflection: My Transformation

Loss changed you.

Cancer changed you.
Healing changed you.
God changed you.
Take time to honor the transformation.

<u>Journal Prompts:</u>

- How am I different now than before my valley?
- What spiritual strengths are now permanent in me?
- What fears have lost their power over me?

7. Reflection: Letting Myself Grieve

You learned a new kind of grief — honest grief, holy grief, permitted grief. You learned that even Jesus wept. This reflection is an invitation to revisit the healing that came through tears.

<u>Journal Prompts:</u>

- How did I allow myself to grieve on this journey?
- What losses resurfaced during this process?
- How did God meet me in my tears?

8. Reflection: Danny's Transformation

This journey didn't just change you — it changed your marriage and your husband's walk with God. His prayers, his tears, his shirts on bell day — all of it was part of God's work.

<u>Journal Prompts:</u>

- How did Danny's faith grow during this journey?
- What moments revealed the Holy Spirit working in him?
- How did our marriage deepen through this season?

9. Reflection: The Miracle of Timing

Nothing was random.
Not the 7th cut.
Not the reduced treatments.
Not the butterfly.

Not the cardinal.
Not the call.
Not the whisper.
Nothing.

<u>Journal Prompts:</u>

- What moments showed me that God was in the timing?
- What would have happened if I acted outside of His timing?
- How has this changed the way I wait on God?

10. Reflection: What I Want to Carry Forward

Healing is not returning to the old version of yourself — it is stepping forward as the healed, restored version. Capture what you never want to forget.

<u>Journal Prompts:</u>

- What lessons do I want to carry into the rest of my life?
- What new habits or spiritual disciplines do I want to maintain?
- What part of my testimony do I want to share with others?

11. Reflection: My Testimony in One Page

Sometimes writing the whole story again helps you see the miracle in it. Summarizing it becomes healing.

<u>Journal Prompts:</u>

- If I could share my testimony in one page, what would I say?
- What is the heart of my story?
- Who needs to hear my testimony?

12. Reflection: My Future with God

This is the moment to step into the *after* with intention.
You are not leaving healing behind —
you are living FROM healing.

<u>Journal Prompts:</u>

- What am I believing God for in the next season of my life?
- What dreams has God awakened in me again?
- What does "faith over fear" look like in my future?

WORSHIP IN THE VALLEY 

(A Devotional Reflection)

"I will bless the Lord at all times: His praise shall continually be in my mouth."
— Psalm 34:1

I used to think worship was something reserved for Sunday morning — the songs, the hands lifted, the familiar rhythm of praise. But cancer taught me something deeper:

Worship is not a moment — it is a weapon.

It is how you breathe when fear tries to suffocate you.

It is how you stand when everything around you feels like sinking sand.

It is how you fight battles you don't have the strength to face.

Worship became my language in the valley.

Not loud, not polished, not perfect —

but heartfelt, desperate, and real.

There were days my hands lifted high in confidence.

There were days my hands lifted high in tears.

There were days I lifted my hands because it was the *only* thing I had strength to lift.

But I lifted them anyway.

I worshiped God through the losses that began in 2022.

Loss after loss — seven losses in two years.

And then the diagnosis in 2025.

It was as if grief and uncertainty were trying to swallow me whole.

But worship kept pulling me back to life.
While others might have turned away from God in pain,
I pressed into Him deeper.
I didn't hide from Him — I ran to Him.
I praised Him through the heartbreak.
I worshiped Him through the waiting.
I surrendered to Him in the unknown.
And God met me in the middle of every song.
Worship was how I survived.
Worship was how I breathed.
Worship was how I fought.

Worship Changes You — and the People Around You
One of the greatest blessings in this journey was witnessing
what worship did to my husband.
As I lifted my hands, he watched.
As I prayed, he listened.
As I praised God through losses, grief, diagnosis, and treatment,
he learned something powerful:
Faith is not proven by circumstances —
faith is proven by consistency.
Danny told me one day,
*"I didn't turn away from God because I watched you run
toward Him. Even when everything around you fell apart,
you held onto Him. That's what made me want to know Him
deeper."*
Worship transformed my home.
It softened my husband's heart.
It strengthened his prayers.
It turned our living room into a sanctuary.
It made our marriage stronger, softer, deeper.
Worship didn't just carry *me* through the valley —
it carried *us*.

Worship Makes Grief Honest
Growing up, my mother never let me see her grieve.
Not when she lost her mother.
Not when life overwhelmed her.
She shielded me from every tear.
So I learned to hide mine.
When I walked through my own losses, I thought I had to be the strong one.
I felt guilty when I cried.
I felt ashamed of my tears.
I thought grief meant I lacked faith.
But then my children — the very ones I was trying to protect —gave *me* permission to grieve.
"Mom, it's okay to cry. You don't have to be strong all the time."
And I remembered something holy:
Jesus wept.
If the Son of God Himself wept,
then surely I didn't have to pretend I was made of steel.
Worship became the place where grief could breathe.
It became where tears turned into testimonies.
It became where pain became praise.

Worship Makes Fear Bow
There were moments when fear overwhelmed me —
moments of waiting for results,
moments before biopsies,
moments on the table,
moments in the dark.
And in those moments, God would give me a song.
Sometimes it was the same verse on repeat.
Sometimes it was a melody with no words.
Sometimes it was a whisper from the Holy Spirit.
But one worship song became my anchor:
"Be still and know."

I wore it on a shirt the day I rang the bell.
It was the Scripture that followed me through every room,
every night,
every moment of fear.
Worship didn't remove the valley —
but it lit the valley.
It turned every scared breath into a sacred one.

Worship Turns Valleys Into Testimony
When I worshiped through my storm, I wasn't just singing.
I was declaring war.
I was resisting the enemy.
I was reminding myself who God is —
and reminding the devil who he is **not.**
Every "Hallelujah" was a strike against fear.
Every worship moment was a declaration of faith.
Every tear lifted in praise was a sacrifice God honored.
Worship was the thread that wove my entire testimony together.

Worship is Not About Perfection — It's About Presence
This journal is not about perfect faith.
It is not about always being strong.
It is not about never crying or never trembling.
It's about **practice** —
practicing surrender,
practicing trust,
practicing obedience,
practicing worship.
Because practice doesn't make perfect.
Practice makes permanent.
Every day I worshiped,
faith became more permanent.
Peace became more permanent.
Trust became more permanent.

God's presence became more permanent.
And that's what carried me — not my strength, but His.

Closing Prayer

*Lord, teach me to worship You in the valley as deeply as I
worship on the mountaintop.*
Let my praise rise even when my knees shake.
Let my song be a weapon when fear tries to return.
*Fill my home, my heart, and my life with a worship that chang-
es atmospheres.*
Let my worship bring You glory —
and let it carry me through every season.
In Jesus' name, amen.

Scripture Appendix

How to Use This Scripture Appendix

This Scripture Appendix is more than a collection of verses — it is a *spiritual toolkit* that God used to carry me through fear, waiting, grief, diagnosis, surgery, radiation, healing, and victory. These pages became my lifeline, and it is my prayer that they become the same for you.

Here are a few ways to use these Scriptures in a way that strengthens your faith and steadies your heart:

1. Read slowly.
These verses are not meant to be rushed.
Take your time.
Let each word sink into your spirit.

2. Read them out loud.
There is power in speaking God's Word.
When your voice declares Scripture, your mind begins to align with truth instead of fear.

3. Pray the prayers after each section.
Every prayer was born from real moments and real tears.
Pray them slowly.
Pray them personally.
Let God meet you through them.

4. Use the declarations with authority.
Your words carry power.

Speak each declaration boldly over your life, your family, your health, and your future.

5. Return to them often.
You will find that different Scriptures speak to you in different seasons.
On days you feel strong, they will fuel your faith.
On days you feel weak, they will breathe life into your spirit.

6. Journal what God reveals.
If a verse stands out, write it down.
If a promise touches you, linger there.
God speaks in layers — keep a journal nearby to capture His whispers.

7. Let these verses become part of your daily rhythm.
Read one category each morning.
Or choose one verse to meditate on throughout the day.
Or pray a Scripture over your family at night.
There is no wrong way to use them — the goal is simply to invite God into your journey.

8. Remember that God meets you in His Word.
These Scriptures carried me through diagnosis, fear, surgeries, radiation, and victory.
They were my breath when I felt overwhelmed.
They were my stability when I felt shaken.
They were my peace when I felt afraid.
May they carry you the same way.
May they become your anchor, your comfort, your strength, and your sanctuary.

As you read these verses, may you feel God's presence draw close, His peace settle over you, and His Word rise up within you — reminding you that you are never walking alone.

Comfort Scriptures (Appendix)

22 Scripture Categories for Every Season

These are the Scriptures that carried me through the hardest days, steadied me in the waiting, and reminded me that God was always near. On the days I felt strong, they became fuel. On the days I felt weak, they became oxygen. On the days fear tried to creep in, they became my weapon.

My prayer is that these verses will anchor your heart the same way they anchored mine — keeping you rooted in truth, wrapped in peace, and covered by God's presence no matter what season you are walking through.

> ***"The grass withereth, the flower fadeth: but the word of our God shall stand for ever."***
> ***— Isaiah 40:8***

God's Word became my anchor, my shield, my steady breath, and my place of peace. These Scriptures carried me through every fear-filled moment, every waiting room, every silent night, and every miracle God performed.

May they now carry you.

Category 1 — When You Are Afraid
(Psalm 56:3, Isaiah 41:10)
Fear rises, but God rises higher.
Declaration: Fear has no place in my story.
Prayer: Lord, quiet fear and strengthen my trust in You.

CATEGORY 2 — WHEN YOU NEED PEACE
(Philippians 4:6–7, John 14:27)
Peace guards the mind like armor.
Declaration: God's peace protects my heart.
Prayer: Let Your peace settle over my spirit.

CATEGORY 3 — WHEN YOU NEED STRENGTH
(Joshua 1:9, Nehemiah 8:10)
Strength is found in surrender, not striving.
Declaration: God is my strength.
Prayer: Empower me where I am weak.

CATEGORY 4 — WHEN YOU NEED HEALING
(Exodus 15:26, Jeremiah 30:17)
God heals body, mind, and spirit.
Declaration: Healing belongs to me.
Prayer: Heal the places I cannot reach.

CATEGORY 5 — WHEN YOU FEEL WEARY
(Isaiah 40:31, Psalm 61:2)
God lifts the weary higher.
Declaration: My strength is renewed in God.
Prayer: Restore my energy and spirit.

CATEGORY 6 — WHEN YOU NEED HOPE
(Romans 8:28, Psalm 27:13)
Hope becomes your lifeline.
Declaration: I expect to see God's goodness.
Prayer: Stir hope in me again.

CATEGORY 7 — WHEN YOU FEEL ALONE
(Hebrews 13:5, Psalm 23:4)
You are never alone in the valley.
Declaration: God is with me in every moment.
Prayer: Surround me with Your presence.

CATEGORY 8 — WHEN YOU NEED GOD'S GUIDANCE
(Proverbs 3:5–6, Psalm 32:8)
God guides the surrendered heart.
Declaration: God directs my steps.
Prayer: Lead me clearly and gently.

CATEGORY 9 — WHEN YOU NEED PROTECTION
(Psalm 91:1–4, Psalm 121:7–8)
God's wings are your refuge.
Declaration: I am covered by God.
Prayer: Surround my home and life with Your protection.

CATEGORY 10 — WHEN YOU NEED GOD TO MOVE
(Ephesians 3:20, Isaiah 65:24)
God moves before you ask.
Declaration: God is making a way for me.
Prayer: Lord, move in ways only You can.

CATEGORY 11 — WHEN YOU NEED GOD'S TIMING
(Ecclesiastes 3:11, Habakkuk 2:3)
God's timing is never wasted.
Declaration: I trust God's timing completely.
Prayer: Help me wait with patience and faith.

CATEGORY 12 — WHEN YOU FEEL OVERWHELMED
(Psalm 61:2, Isaiah 40:29)
God lifts you above the waves.
Declaration: God is my stability.
Prayer: Lift me to the Rock higher than me.

CATEGORY 13 — WHEN YOU FEEL UNWORTHY
(Romans 5:8, Psalm 103:10–12)
Grace covers every insecurity.
Declaration: I am deeply loved by God.
Prayer: Replace shame with Your truth.

CATEGORY 14 — WHEN YOU NEED RESTORATION
(Psalm 23:3, Joel 2:25)
God restores what life has broken.
Declaration: God restores my soul.
Prayer: Restore what loss has taken.

CATEGORY 15 — WHEN YOU NEED DELIVERANCE
(Psalm 34:17, Nahum 1:7)
God breaks chains gently and powerfully.
Declaration: I am delivered and protected.
Prayer: Free me from anything that holds me captive.

CATEGORY 16 — WHEN YOU NEED PATIENCE
(Psalm 37:7, Lamentations 3:25)
Patience is faith stretched thin but still standing.
Declaration: Waiting makes me stronger.
Prayer: Help me wait with grace.

CATEGORY 17 — WHEN YOU'RE BATTLING ANXIETY
(1 Peter 5:7, Philippians 4:8)
Anxiety weakens where truth strengthens.
Declaration: I cast all anxiety onto God.
Prayer: Replace fearful thoughts with Your peace.

CATEGORY 18 — WHEN YOU NEED BREAKTHROUGH
(Micah 2:13, Isaiah 45:2)
God is the Breaker who goes before you.
Declaration: Breakthrough is coming.
Prayer: Break every barrier in Your name.

CATEGORY 19 — WHEN YOU'RE WALKING THROUGH LOSS
(Psalm 30:11, Psalm 34:18)
God meets you in the ache.
Declaration: God is near my broken heart.
Prayer: Heal the places touched by grief.

CATEGORY 20 — WHEN YOU'RE LEARNING TO TRUST AGAIN

(Proverbs 3:5, Psalm 56:3)

Trust is rebuilt one surrender at a time.

Declaration: I trust God deeper each day.

Prayer: Teach me to trust again.

CATEGORY 21 — WHEN YOU NEED RESURRECTION HOPE

(John 11:25, Romans 8:11)

The same power that raised Jesus is working in you.

Declaration: Resurrection power lives in me.

Prayer: Bring new life where things have felt dead.

CATEGORY 22 — WHEN GOD CALLS YOU TO BE STILL

(Psalm 46:10, Isaiah 30:15, 1 Kings 19:12)

Stillness is not inactivity — it is trust.

Quietness is where God speaks.

Silence is where strength rises.

Declaration: Stillness is my strength and sanctuary.

Prayer: Quiet my soul and let me hear Your whisper.

 WHEN YOU ARE AFRAID

Isaiah 41:10

"Fear thou not; for I am with thee..."

Fear is loud, but God's presence is louder.

This verse reminds us that fear doesn't get to be our guide — God does. When anxiety tries to rise, this Scripture becomes a shield around your heart. It tells you that you are not alone, not abandoned, and not unprotected.

Declaration:

I refuse to fear, because God is with me. His presence is my peace.

Prayer:

Lord, quiet every fear and remind me that You walk with me, fight for me, and hold me close. Amen.

Psalm 56:3

"What time I am afraid, I will trust in thee."

Trust is a choice, not a feeling.

Even when our emotions tremble, God remains steady. This Scripture is permission to bring your fear to God — not hide it — and trust Him right in the middle of it.

Declaration:

When fear rises, faith rises higher.

Prayer:

God, when I feel afraid, help me turn to You first. Strengthen my trust in Your goodness. Amen.

🖋 WHEN YOU NEED PEACE

Philippians 4:6–7

"Be careful for nothing... and the peace of God... shall keep your hearts and minds..."

God's peace isn't the absence of trouble — it's the presence of Christ in the trouble.

This peace protects your mind like armor, guarding you from worry and the pressure of the unknown.

Declaration:

God's peace guards my heart and mind.

Prayer:

Lord, settle my spirit and let Your peace wash over every anxious thought. Amen.

John 14:27

"Let not your heart be troubled..."

Jesus didn't say trouble wouldn't come — He said we don't have to let it in.

This verse calls us to resist fear's intrusion and stand under the peace God has promised.

Declaration:

My heart belongs to God, not to worry.

Prayer:

Jesus, calm the storms inside me and breathe peace into the parts of me that feel unsettled. Amen.

🖋 WHEN YOU NEED STRENGTH

Joshua 1:9

"Be strong and of a good courage..."

Strength isn't the absence of weakness — it's God's power in your weakness.

This Scripture reminds you that courage is not something you muster up — it's something God gives.

Declaration:

God strengthens me for every step ahead.

Prayer:

Lord, fill me with courage. Make me strong in the places where I feel weak. Amen.

Nehemiah 8:10

"The joy of the Lord is your strength."

Joy is a weapon — not a mood.

Even when life feels heavy, God gives joy that lifts, renews, and carries you.

Declaration:

God's joy fuels my strength.

Prayer:

Father, restore joy to my heart and let it become strength in my spirit. Amen.

🖋 WHEN YOU NEED HEALING

Exodus 15:26

"For I am the Lord that healeth thee."

Healing is part of God's identity.

He doesn't just heal bodies — He heals hearts, minds, and memories.

Declaration:

God is my healer. I receive His healing in every part of my life.

Prayer:

Jehovah Rapha, thank You for healing me — physically, spiritually, and emotionally. Amen.

Jeremiah 30:17

"For I will restore health unto thee..."

Restoration is God's specialty.

He restores what sickness steals. He restores what fear damages. He restores what trauma disrupts.

Declaration:

God restores every broken place.

Prayer:
Lord, restore me fully — in ways only You can. Amen.

🪶 WHEN YOU FEEL WEARY

Isaiah 40:31
"They that wait upon the Lord shall renew their strength..."
Waiting isn't wasted.
In the waiting, God renews, refills, and revives.
Declaration:
My strength is renewed as I wait on God.
Prayer:
Father, renew my strength in the waiting. Lift me up on wings like eagles. Amen.

Psalm 61:2
"When my heart is overwhelmed... lead me to the rock that is higher than I."
When the world feels too heavy, God lifts you above the weight of it.
He becomes the Rock you stand on when your own footing feels unsteady.
Declaration:
God is higher than anything that overwhelms me.
Prayer:
Lord, lift me above the waves and anchor me in Your stability. Amen.

🪶 WHEN YOU NEED HOPE

Romans 8:28
"All things work together for good..."
Nothing is wasted with God.
Not pain.
Not waiting.
Not tears.
Not diagnosis.
He weaves them into purpose.
Declaration:
God is working all things for my good.

Prayer:
Lord, help me see Your hand even when I do not see the whole plan. Amen.

Psalm 27:13
"I had fainted, unless I had believed to see the goodness of the Lord..."
Hope keeps you standing.
Hope looks forward.
Hope expects God's goodness.
Declaration:
I expect to see God's goodness in my life.
Prayer:
Father, fill my heart with expectancy. Let hope rise again. Amen.

🖋 WHEN YOU FEEL ALONE

Hebrews 13:5
"I will never leave thee, nor forsake thee."
God never abandons His children.
Not in hospital rooms.
Not in waiting rooms.
Not in quiet bedrooms.
Not in valleys.
Declaration:
I am never alone — God is always with me.
Prayer:
Lord, let Your nearness become my comfort. Amen.

Psalm 23:4
"Yea, though I walk through the valley... Thou art with me."
God doesn't let you walk through valleys alone — He walks *with* you.
Your fear may whisper otherwise, but valleys always reveal God's closeness.
Declaration:
God walks with me in every valley.

Prayer:

Shepherd of my soul, walk beside me today and calm every fear. Amen.

WHEN YOU NEED REMINDERS OF GOD'S LOVE

Romans 8:38–39

"Nothing... shall be able to separate us from the love of God..."
Nothing — not sickness, not fear, not a hard diagnosis — can separate you from God's love.

Declaration:

God's love holds me securely.

Prayer:

Lord, wrap me in Your love and let it cast out all fear. Amen.

Zephaniah 3:17

"He will rejoice over thee with joy... He will quiet thee with his love."
God's love doesn't just save — it quiets.
It settles.
It soothes.

Declaration:

God sings over me with love.

Prayer:

Father, quiet my heart with Your love today. Amen.

WHEN YOU NEED COURAGE FOR THE UNKNOWN

Isaiah 43:2

"When thou passest through the waters, I will be with thee..."
The unknown is frightening because it's uncontrollable.
But God never sends you into the deep without going before you.
He does not promise a life without deep waters —
He promises His presence *in* them.

Declaration:

I will not fear the unknown, because God is already there.

Prayer:
Lord, walk beside me in every place my fear imagines. Remind me that You go before me. Amen.

Deuteronomy 31:8
"He will be with thee, he will not fail thee..."
This is not a suggestion or a possibility — it is a promise.
God cannot fail.
He cannot abandon.
He cannot forget.
He holds the future, and He holds you.
Declaration:
God is in my tomorrow just as surely as He is in my today.
Prayer:
Father, strengthen my confidence in Your faithful presence. Help me trust Your leading. Amen.

Psalm 112:7
"He shall not be afraid of evil tidings: his heart is fixed, trusting in the Lord."
A fixed heart cannot be shaken.
It is rooted, anchored, established in Christ.
Declaration:
My heart is fixed. Trusting God is my stability.
Prayer:
Lord, steady my heart when fear tries to return. Anchor me in Your truth. Amen.

WHEN YOU NEED GOD'S GUIDANCE

Proverbs 3:5–6
"Trust in the Lord with all thine heart... and he shall direct thy paths."
Surrender activates direction.
The more we release, the more clearly we hear.
Declaration:
God is directing my steps — I will follow without fear.

Prayer:
Guide me, Lord. Make my path straight and my spirit willing. Amen.

Psalm 32:8
"I will instruct thee and teach thee... I will guide thee with mine eye."
God teaches you gently —
not through panic, but through peace.
Not through confusion, but through clarity.
Declaration:
God Himself is my teacher, my guide, and my counselor.
Prayer:
Father, teach me Your ways and help me recognize Your voice. Amen.

James 1:5
"If any of you lack wisdom, let him ask of God..."
Wisdom is not earned — it's received.
And God gives it generously, without hesitation or judgment.
Declaration:
God gives me wisdom freely and faithfully.
Prayer:
Lord, give me wisdom beyond my understanding. Amen.

🪶 WHEN YOU NEED PROTECTION

Psalm 91:1–4
"He shall cover thee with his feathers..."
This is one of the most comforting passages in Scripture.
It shows God not as distant, but as protective, nurturing, shielding, covering.
Declaration:
I am covered. I am hidden. I am protected under God's wings.
Prayer:
Lord, cover me with Your feathers and let me find refuge under Your wings. Amen.

2 Thessalonians 3:3
"The Lord is faithful, who shall stablish you, and keep you from evil."
He doesn't just protect your body —
He protects your mind, your spirit, your peace, your future.
Declaration:
The Lord keeps me from harm and strengthens me in every season.
Prayer:
Faithful God, surround me with Your protection and guard my heart from every attack. Amen.

Psalm 121:7–8
"The Lord shall preserve thee from all evil..."
Not some.
Not most.
All.
Declaration:
God preserves me coming in and going out.
Prayer:
Lord, preserve my life, my health, my mind, and my purpose. Amen.

🪶 WHEN YOU NEED GOD'S PRESENCE

Psalm 16:11
"In thy presence is fulness of joy..."
Joy is not found in circumstances —
it is found in Him.
Declaration:
God's presence is my joy, my rest, and my refuge.
Prayer:
Lord, draw me near. Let Your presence be the atmosphere of my life. Amen.

Psalm 139:7–10
"Whither shall I go from thy spirit?"
You cannot outrun His presence.

You cannot hide from His love.
You cannot fall outside His reach.
Declaration:
God is with me, beside me, before me, and behind me.
Prayer:
Father, let me sense Your presence in every moment. Amen.

Zephaniah 3:17
"He will joy over thee with singing."
Imagine that —
God sings over you.
He delights in you.
Declaration:
God sings over me with love and joy.
Prayer:
Lord, quiet me with Your love today. Amen.

🪶 WHEN YOU FEEL BROKEN OR WEAK

Psalm 147:3
"He healeth the broken in heart..."
There is no heartbreak too deep for God to mend.
Declaration:
God is healing every part of me — seen and unseen.
Prayer:
Lord, mend the broken pieces of my heart. Restore what pain has damaged. Amen.

2 Corinthians 12:9
"My strength is made perfect in weakness."
Weakness isn't failure —
it's an invitation for God to show His power.
Declaration:
God's strength is perfected in my weakness.
Prayer:
Father, let Your strength rise where mine ends. Amen.

Psalm 34:18
"The Lord is nigh unto them that are of a broken heart."
God is closest when you feel most fragile.
Declaration:
God is near me in my brokenness.
Prayer:
Lord, draw near and hold me close in moments when I feel overwhelmed. Amen.

🪶 WHEN YOU NEED GOD TO MOVE

Ephesians 3:20
"Exceeding abundantly above all that we ask or think..."
God doesn't answer prayers with "just enough."
He answers **abundantly**.
Declaration:
God is doing more than I can ask, think, or imagine.
Prayer:
Lord, move in ways that show Your glory and surpass my expectations. Amen.

Isaiah 65:24
"Before they call, I will answer..."
God is already working on what you have not yet prayed.
Declaration:
God knows, God sees, God responds — before I even ask.
Prayer:
Thank You for answering prayers I haven't spoken yet. Amen.

Mark 11:24
"What things soever ye desire, when ye pray, believe..."
Faith isn't belief in outcomes —
it's belief in the God who gives them.
Declaration:
I believe God hears, responds, and answers according to His will.

Prayer:

Lord, help my unbelief and strengthen my faith to believe You boldly. Amen.

🖋 WHEN YOU NEED HOPE FOR THE FUTURE

Jeremiah 29:11

"Thoughts of peace, and not of evil..."

God's plans for you are good —

even when current circumstances don't feel good yet.

Declaration:

My future is held in the hands of a good God.

Prayer:

Lord, give me eyes to see the hope You have woven into my future. Amen.

Romans 15:13

"The God of hope fill you with all joy and peace in believing..."

Hope fills.

Hope sustains.

Hope steadies.

Declaration:

I overflow with hope through the power of the Holy Spirit.

Prayer:

Holy Spirit, fill me with hope that overflows into every part of my life. Amen.

Psalm 126:5

"They that sow in tears shall reap in joy."

Your tears have purpose.

Your pain has harvest.

Your sorrow has a future filled with joy.

Declaration:

My tears are not wasted — God is turning them into joy.

Prayer:

Father, turn my mourning into dancing and my tears into testimonies. Amen.

🖋 WHEN YOU NEED REST

Matthew 11:28–29

"Come unto me, all ye that labour and are heavy laden, and I will give you rest."

Rest is not something you earn — it is something you receive. And God does not offer temporary rest; He offers deep, soul-level rest that carries you through storms and into peace. When everything around you feels heavy, God invites you to lay it down, not carry it.

Declaration:

I receive God's rest. My soul is safe, still, and held.

Prayer:

Lord, lift the weight from my shoulders and quiet my spirit. Give me the rest only You can provide. Amen.

Psalm 4:8

"I will both lay me down in peace, and sleep…"
Sleep during a storm is a miracle in itself.
When God fills your mind with peace, your nights become sanctuaries. Even when circumstances don't change, His peace changes *you.*

Declaration:

My sleep is blessed, peaceful, and protected by God.

Prayer:

Father, grant me peaceful rest tonight. Cover my mind and give me deep, healing sleep. Amen.

🖋 WHEN YOU FEEL OVERWHELMED

Psalm 61:2

"When my heart is overwhelmed: lead me to the rock that is higher than I."
Overwhelm hits fast — but God lifts you faster.
He raises you above what tries to drown you and places your feet on higher ground.

Declaration:

God lifts me above overwhelm and anchors me in His stability.

Prayer:
Lord, lead me higher than my feelings. Lift me above the weight pressing on my spirit. Amen.

Isaiah 40:29
"He giveth power to the faint..."
God gives power where you lack it.
He strengthens you where you feel weakest.
Declaration:
God is my strength when I have none.
Prayer:
Strengthen me, God. Replace my weariness with Your supernatural power. Amen.

🪶 WHEN YOU FEEL UNWORTHY

Romans 5:8
"While we were yet sinners, Christ died for us."
Nothing about God's love is based on your performance.
You are loved because He chose to love you — not because you earned it.
Declaration:
God's love defines me — not my mistakes.
Prayer:
Father, remind me that I am loved, seen, and chosen. Amen.

Psalm 103:10–12
"He hath not dealt with us after our sins..."
God doesn't measure you by your past — He washes it clean.
Guilt is not your identity.
Shame is not your inheritance.
Declaration:
I am forgiven, redeemed, and deeply loved by God.
Prayer:
Lord, remove shame from my heart and replace it with Your truth. Amen.

🖋 WHEN YOU NEED GOD'S TIMING

Ecclesiastes 3:11
"He hath made every thing beautiful in his time..."
God's timing is never rushed and never late.
He sees the whole picture when we only see a single moment.
Declaration:
I trust God's timing — it is perfect and purposeful.
Prayer:
Lord, still my impatience and help me wait with faith. Amen.

Habakkuk 2:3
"Though it tarry, wait for it..."
Delay is not denial.
If God promised it, it WILL come.
Declaration:
I will wait in expectation, not frustration.
Prayer:
Teach me to wait with hope, knowing Your timing is always right. Amen.

🖋 WHEN YOU NEED RESTORATION

Psalm 23:3
"He restoreth my soul..."
Restoration means more than repair — it means renewed life.
God restores what fear drains and what sorrow scatters.
Declaration:
God restores my soul, my peace, and my joy.
Prayer:
Restore me, Lord. Make whole what has been bruised or broken. Amen.

Joel 2:25
"I will restore to you the years..."
God restores lost time, lost opportunities, lost seasons.
Nothing is wasted when God restores it.

Declaration:
God restores everything I thought was lost.
Prayer:
Lord, bring restoration to every area touched by pain. Amen.

🪶 WHEN YOU NEED DELIVERANCE

Psalm 34:17
"The righteous cry, and the Lord heareth, and delivereth them..."
Deliverance is God's specialty.
He pulls you out of fear, anxiety, and emotional heaviness with His mighty hand.
Declaration:
God delivers me from every fear and every attack.
Prayer:
Deliver me, Lord, from anything that tries to hold me captive. Amen.

Nahum 1:7
"He knoweth them that trust in him."
God doesn't just deliver — He protects, shields, and covers His children.
Declaration:
I am covered and protected by God's deliverance.
Prayer:
Lord, be my refuge and deliverer in every battle. Amen.

🪶 WHEN YOU NEED PATIENCE

Psalm 37:7
"Rest in the Lord, and wait patiently for him..."
Patience is not passive — it's faith in motion.
It's trusting God's unseen hands.
Declaration:
I wait with faith, not frustration.

Prayer:
Lord, teach me patience as You unfold Your plan. Amen.

Lamentations 3:25
"The Lord is good unto them that wait for him..."
Waiting is not punishment — it is preparation.
Declaration:
Waiting makes me stronger, not weaker.
Prayer:
Help me embrace Your timing with grace and trust. Amen.

🖋 WHEN YOU NEED JOY AGAIN

Psalm 30:5
"Joy cometh in the morning."
Morning doesn't always come when the sun rises —
it comes when God lifts your spirit.
Declaration:
My joy is returning, one breath at a time.
Prayer:
Lord, restore joy where sorrow has lived too long. Amen.

Psalm 16:11
"In thy presence is fulness of joy..."
Joy is not found in circumstances — it is found in Him.
Declaration:
Joy is my portion because God is my source.
Prayer:
Fill me with joy that goes deeper than situations. Amen.

🖋 WHEN YOU NEED GOD TO FIGHT FOR YOU

Exodus 14:14
"The Lord shall fight for you..."
Some battles are not yours to fight —
they belong to God.

Declaration:
God fights for me — I will hold my peace.
Prayer:
Lord, fight the battles I cannot fight. Amen.

2 Chronicles 20:17
"Stand ye still, and see the salvation of the Lord..."
Your victory is not earned — it is witnessed.
Declaration:
I will stand still and watch God move.
Prayer:
Strengthen my faith to stand still and trust You fully. Amen.

WHEN YOU NEED WISDOM

James 1:5
"If any of you lack wisdom, let him ask of God... and it shall be given him."
God never shames your need for answers.
Wisdom is not earned — it is gifted.
You don't have to stumble in confusion or guess your way through life.
God gives wisdom freely, generously, and without holding anything back.
Declaration:
God gives me wisdom without hesitation.
Prayer:
Lord, open my understanding. Guide my decisions and show me Your way. Amen.

Proverbs 2:6
"For the Lord giveth wisdom..."
True wisdom does not come from education, age, or experience.
It comes from God Himself.
Declaration:
The Lord is my source of wisdom and understanding.
Prayer:
Father, help me hear Your voice above all others. Teach me Your wisdom. Amen.

🖋 WHEN YOU'RE WAITING ON TEST RESULTS

Psalm 46:10
"Be still, and know that I am God."
There is no stillness like the stillness in a waiting room.
But God meets you even there.
Waiting does not mean uncertainty — waiting means God is working.
Declaration:
In the waiting, I will be still and trust God fully.
Prayer:
Lord, calm my mind as I wait. Strengthen my heart and let Your peace settle me. Amen.

Isaiah 40:31
"They that wait upon the Lord shall renew their strength..."
Waiting is not a pause in your journey —
it is a place where God renews and refills your strength.
Declaration:
My strength is renewed as I wait on God.
Prayer:
Father, help me wait with faith instead of fear. Amen.

🖋 WHEN YOU'RE BATTLING ANXIETY

1 Peter 5:7
"Casting all your care upon him; for he careth for you."
Anxiety is a weight you were never meant to carry alone.
God invites — even commands — you to cast it onto Him.
Declaration:
I cast all my anxiety onto God because He cares deeply for me.
Prayer:
Lord, take every anxious thought and replace it with Your peace. Amen.

Philippians 4:8
"Think on these things..."
Anxiety fills your mind with what-if's.

God fills your mind with whatever is true, lovely, pure, and praiseworthy.
Declaration:
My mind focuses on the things of God, not the lies of fear.
Prayer:
Father, redirect my thoughts toward Your truth and Your goodness. Amen.

🪶 WHEN YOU NEED EMOTIONAL HEALING

Psalm 147:3
"He healeth the broken in heart..."
God heals more than bodies —
He heals hearts.
He meets you in the wounds no one else sees.
Declaration:
God heals every part of my heart — even the hidden places.
Prayer:
Lord, restore the places in me that have been wounded by life. Amen.

Jeremiah 17:14
"Heal me, O Lord, and I shall be healed..."
When God heals, it is complete —
spiritual, emotional, and physical healing are all tied to His presence.
Declaration:
God's healing reaches every level of my being.
Prayer:
Father, touch my heart and heal what I do not know how to express. Amen.

🪶 WHEN GOD SEEMS SILENT

Psalm 13:1–2
"How long wilt thou forget me, O Lord?"
Even David felt forgotten sometimes.
Silence does not mean distance —
it means God is working in ways you cannot see.

Declaration:

God is working behind the scenes even when I hear nothing.

Prayer:

Lord, strengthen me in Your silence and remind me You are near. Amen.

Psalm 27:14

"Wait on the Lord... and he shall strengthen thine heart."

God uses silence to strengthen, not punish.

Declaration:

I will wait for God with courage and expectation.

Prayer:

Father, give me patience to wait with confidence in Your plan. Amen.

🖋 WHEN YOU NEED TO RELEASE CONTROL

Proverbs 16:3

"Commit thy works unto the Lord..."

Letting go is an act of trust.

Releasing control is admitting that God knows better, sees further, and loves deeper.

Declaration:

I release control and surrender every detail to God.

Prayer:

Lord, take what I am holding too tightly. Help me rest in Your control. Amen.

Psalm 37:5

"Commit thy way unto the Lord; trust also in him..."

Surrender is not weakness.

It is wisdom.

Declaration:

My life is committed to the One who knows my beginning and my end.

Prayer:
Father, I trust You with what I cannot fix, control, or understand. Amen.

🖋 WHEN YOU NEED A BREAKTHROUGH

Micah 2:13
"The breaker has come up before them..."
God is the Breaker —
the One who goes ahead, breaks through barriers, and opens paths.
Declaration:
My Breaker goes before me and makes the impossible possible.
Prayer:
Lord, go before me and break through every wall and obstacle. Amen.

Isaiah 45:2
"I will go before thee, and make the crooked places straight..."
God levels mountains, straightens paths, and opens locked doors.
Declaration:
God is making my path clear, open, and victorious.
Prayer:
Father, create a breakthrough in the areas where I feel stuck. Amen.

🖋 WHEN YOU FEEL SPIRITUALLY ATTACKED

Isaiah 54:17
"No weapon formed against thee shall prosper..."
Weapons may form —
diagnosis may come,
fear may rise,
conflict may show up —
but they will NOT prosper.
Declaration:
Every weapon formed against me fails in Jesus' name.

Prayer:

Lord, cover me in Your protection and dismantle every attack of the enemy. Amen.

2 Corinthians 10:4

"The weapons of our warfare are not carnal..."
You are equipped with divine weapons —
Scripture, prayer, worship, and the Holy Spirit.
Declaration:
I fight my battles with spiritual strength, not fleshly fear.
Prayer:
Father, help me use the spiritual weapons You've given me. Amen.

WHEN YOU NEED COURAGE TO HOPE AGAIN

Psalm 31:24

"Be of good courage, and he shall strengthen your heart..."
Hope requires courage after disappointment.
God strengthens your heart to believe again.
Declaration:
God strengthens my heart to hope boldly.
Prayer:
Lord, give me courage to hope again — and to expect Your goodness. Amen.

Romans 8:25

"But if we hope for that we see not, then do we with patience wait for it."
Hope for what you **cannot see** is faith in motion.
Declaration:
My hope is alive because God is faithful.
Prayer:
Holy Spirit, breathe hope into every weary place inside me. Amen.

✒ WHEN YOU FEEL GRIEF RISING

Psalm 34:18
"The Lord is nigh unto them that are of a broken heart..."
Grief is heavy, unexpected, and unpredictable. But God draws *closer* in grief, not further away. He does not shame your tears — He collects them.
Declaration:
God is near me in my grief and comforts every broken place.
Prayer:
Lord, sit with me in the moments when sorrow feels overwhelming. Hold my heart gently. Amen.

Revelation 21:4
"And God shall wipe away all tears..."
Every tear has an expiration date. Grief may linger, but healing is promised.
Declaration:
God is wiping away the tears that sorrow created.
Prayer:
Father, wipe away my tears and replace them with Your peace. Amen.

✒ WHEN YOU FEEL GOD ASKING YOU TO LET GO

Philippians 3:13
"Forgetting those things which are behind..."
Letting go isn't forgetting — it's releasing your grip so God can fill your hands with something better.
Declaration:
I release what weighs me down and hold on to what God has for me.
Prayer:
Lord, help me let go of what You've asked me to release. Amen.

Isaiah 43:18–19
"Behold, I will do a new thing..."

New things require empty hands.
And God never removes without replacing.
Declaration:
I embrace the new things God is doing in my life.
Prayer:
Father, prepare my heart for the new seasons You are leading me into. Amen.

✒ WHEN YOU NEED GOD TO OPEN A DOOR

Revelation 3:8
"Behold, I have set before thee an open door..."
If God opens it, no one can shut it.
If He shuts it, no one can pry it open.
Declaration:
God is opening doors designed specifically for me.
Prayer:
Lord, open the doors You've ordained and close the ones that are not for me. Amen.

Psalm 84:11
"No good thing will he withhold..."
If God withholds something, it is not good *for now.*
His timing protects you.
Declaration:
God withholds no good thing from me according to His perfect wisdom.
Prayer:
Father, help me trust that Your "not yet" is still love. Amen.

✒ WHEN YOU NEED GOD TO MAKE A WAY

Isaiah 43:16
"Thus saith the Lord... which maketh a way in the sea..."
God specializes in impossible paths — He creates roads where none exist.

Declaration:
God is making a way for me even where I cannot see one.
Prayer:
Lord, show me the path You are carving for my life. Amen.

Proverbs 3:6
"In all thy ways acknowledge him, and he shall direct thy paths."
Acknowledging God invites alignment.
Declaration:
God directs every step I take.
Prayer:
Father, guide my path clearly and gently. Amen.

🪶 WHEN YOU NEED GOD TO REMOVE FEAR FROM YOUR MIND

2 Timothy 1:7
"For God hath not given us the spirit of fear..."
Fear is not from God, so it has no right to stay.
Declaration:
Fear is not my portion — peace is.
Prayer:
Lord, evict every trace of fear from my mind and fill me with Your peace. Amen.

1 John 4:18
"Perfect love casteth out fear..."
When love enters, fear exits.
God does not share space with fear.
Declaration:
The love of God drives out every fear in me.
Prayer:
Father, overwhelm my heart with Your perfect love. Amen.

🪶 WHEN YOU NEED FAITH TO RISE AGAIN

Mark 9:23–24
"Lord, I believe; help thou mine unbelief."
Faith and doubt can coexist —
but God grows the faith and heals the doubt.
Declaration:
I believe, and God strengthens every place in me that doubts.
Prayer:
Lord, help my unbelief. Strengthen my faith in Your goodness.
Amen.

Hebrews 11:6
"Without faith it is impossible to please him..."
Faith pleases God — not because it is perfect, but because it
trusts His character.
Declaration:
My faith pleases God because it rests in who He is.
Prayer:
Father, increase my faith. Teach me to trust You fully. Amen.

🪶 WHEN YOU FEEL SPIRITUALLY DRY

Psalm 42:1–2
"As the hart panteth after the water brooks..."
A thirsty soul is a sign that God is calling you deeper.
Dry seasons are invitations, not punishments.
Declaration:
God is refreshing every dry place in my soul.
Prayer:
Lord, quench my spiritual thirst and draw me closer to You.
Amen.

John 7:38
"Out of his belly shall flow rivers of living water."
God does not offer drops — He offers rivers.

Declaration:
Living water flows through me, refreshing my spirit.
Prayer:
Father, fill me with Your life-giving Spirit again. Amen.

🖋 WHEN YOU FEEL CONFUSED

1 Corinthians 14:33
"For God is not the author of confusion..."
Confusion is not from God — clarity is.
Declaration:
I reject confusion and receive God's clarity.
Prayer:
Lord, bring order to my thoughts and peace to my mind. Amen.

Psalm 119:130
"The entrance of thy words giveth light..."
Light ends confusion.
Scripture brings understanding.
Declaration:
God's Word lights my path and brings clarity to my spirit.
Prayer:
Father, shine light on the places where confusion has settled.
Amen.

🖋 WHEN YOU FEEL GOD IS CALLING YOU TO SOMETHING NEW

Joshua 1:2
"Arise, go over this Jordan..."
There comes a moment when God says, "Move."
New assignments require new courage.
Declaration:
I am rising into the new season God is calling me into.
Prayer:
Lord, give me courage to step into the new chapter You have
prepared. Amen.

Isaiah 60:1

"Arise, shine; for thy light is come..."

Your new season is not random — it is revealed by God.

Declaration:

I arise and shine because God's light is upon me.

Prayer:

Father, help me embrace every new thing You're bringing into my life. Amen.

🖋 WHEN YOU'RE WALKING THROUGH LOSS

Psalm 30:11

"Thou hast turned for me my mourning into dancing..."

Loss shakes your heart in ways nothing else can.

But even in mourning, God is quietly working —

turning sorrow into strength,

pain into purpose,

and tears into testimonies.

You don't have to pretend you're okay.

You don't have to rush your healing.

You don't have to hide your grief.

Jesus wept.

And if the Savior of the world made space for grief,

you can too.

Declaration:

God is turning my mourning into dancing, and my grief into joy.

Prayer:

Lord, hold me in the places where my heart feels shattered. Heal me gently. Restore joy in Your perfect time. Amen.

Psalm 34:18

"The Lord is nigh unto them that are of a broken heart..."

God is closest when your heart feels the farthest away from strength.

He sits with you, He comforts you, He collects your tears.
Declaration:
God is near me in loss — I am not alone.
Prayer:
Father, comfort the broken places in me and fill them with Your peace. Amen.

🪶 WHEN YOU NEED GOD TO SPEAK

Jeremiah 33:3
"Call unto me, and I will answer thee..."
God is not silent — He is strategic.
His voice comes in whispers, in Scripture, in signs, in stillness.
When God speaks, everything shifts — not always your situation, but always your spirit.
When you long to hear His voice, keep calling.
He has never failed to answer.
Declaration:
God speaks to me, and I will listen for His whisper.
Prayer:
Lord, open my ears and quiet my thoughts so I can hear You clearly. Amen.

Psalm 85:8
"I will hear what God the Lord will speak..."
Hearing God starts with a willing heart.
When you lean in, He leans closer.
Declaration:
I am attentive to the voice of God and open to His guidance.
Prayer:
Father, speak peace to my heart and direction to my steps. Amen.

🪶 WHEN YOU'RE LEARNING TO TRUST AGAIN

Proverbs 3:5
"Trust in the Lord with all thine heart..."

Trust is not instant — it's built, stretched, rebuilt, and reinforced over time.

Your heart may tremble, but your spirit can still trust.

Trust grows every time you:

- surrender a fear
- let go of a burden
- pray instead of panic
- worship instead of worry

Declaration:
I trust God with all my heart, even when I don't understand.
Prayer:
Lord, teach me to trust You deeper, stronger, and more fully every day. Amen.

Psalm 56:3
"What time I am afraid, I will trust in thee."
Trust and fear can coexist —
but trust is the part that wins.
Declaration:
I choose trust over fear in every situation.
Prayer:
Father, steady my heart where it wavers and teach me to trust You completely. Amen.

🪶 WHEN YOU NEED RESURRECTION HOPE
(Perfect for the woman who fears death, diagnosis, or the unknown)

John 11:25
"I am the resurrection, and the life..."
Resurrection isn't just about eternity —
it's about today.
God resurrects:

- hope
- strength

- joy
- purpose
- peace
- dreams you thought were dead

Cancer does not have the final word.

Fear does not have the final word.

Loss does not have the final word.

Jesus does.

Declaration:

The resurrection power of Jesus lives in me — nothing in my life is beyond His reach.

Prayer:

Lord, resurrect what has died inside me and breathe new life into every weary place. Amen.

Romans 8:11

"He that raised up Christ from the dead shall also quicken your mortal bodies..."

The same power that raised Jesus is alive in you.

There is no situation too dark, no diagnosis too strong, no valley too deep.

Declaration:

God's resurrection power is working in my body, mind, and spirit.

Prayer:

Father, bring life, strength, and renewal to every part of me by Your Spirit. Amen.

Closing Sections

FINAL BENEDICTION

May the Lord bless you and keep you.

May His face shine upon you and give you peace.

May His presence go before you, behind you, beside you, and within you.

May every fear bow to His love.

May every uncertainty bow to His sovereignty.

May every sickness bow to His healing power.

May every tear bow to His joy.

May your valley become your testimony.

May your pain become your purpose.

May your weakness become the place where His strength is revealed.

As you continue your own journey, may God whisper to your heart:

"I am with you."

When fear rises,
may faith rise higher.

When darkness presses in,
may His light guide your steps.

When you feel alone,
may you sense His arms around you.

When you feel weary,
may His Spirit renew your strength.

I speak peace over your mind,
healing over your body,
courage over your decisions,

and hope over your future.
May the God of all grace,
who has carried me through every valley,
carry you through every step of your journey.
In Jesus' name,
Amen.

EPILOGUE PRAYER — SPEAKING LIFE OVER YOUR JOURNEY

Lord, thank You for every promise in Your Word.
Thank You that these Scriptures are alive, powerful, and anchored in Your faithfulness.
Let every verse continue to speak, comfort, strengthen, and guide.
Let fear bow to faith,
sickness bow to healing,
and sorrow bow to joy.
May every person who reads these Scriptures feel Your presence,
Your peace,
Your power,
and Your love.
In Jesus' name, amen.

God's Presence in the Storm

• **Isaiah 41:10** – "Fear thou not; for I am with thee: be not dismayed; for I am thy God: I will strengthen thee; yea, I will help thee; yea, I will uphold thee with the right hand of my righteousness."

• **Hebrews 13:5** – "I will never leave thee, nor forsake thee."

• **Psalm 46:1** – "God is our refuge and strength, a very present help in trouble."

These Scriptures reminded me that God was not watching from a distance — He was beside me, holding my hand, steadying my heart, and covering me with His peace.

Peace Over Fear

• **Philippians 4:6–7** – "Be careful for nothing; but in every thing by prayer and supplication with thanksgiving let your requests be made known unto God. And the peace of God, which passeth all understanding, shall keep your hearts and minds through Christ Jesus."

• **John 14:27** – "Peace I leave with you, my peace I give unto you... Let not your heart be troubled, neither let it be afraid."

• **2 Timothy 1:7** – "For God hath not given us the spirit of fear; but of power, and of love, and of a sound mind."

When anxiety tried to whisper, these verses shouted louder.

Strength and Courage

• **Joshua 1:9** – "Be strong and of a good courage... for the Lord thy God is with thee whithersoever thou goest."

• **Nehemiah 8:10** – "For the joy of the Lord is your strength."

• **Psalm 27:14** – "Wait on the Lord: be of good courage, and he shall strengthen thine heart..."

These Scriptures gave me strength when I felt none — a reminder that courage is not the absence of fear, but the presence of God.

God's Healing Promises

• **Exodus 15:26** – "For I am the Lord that healeth thee."

• **Jeremiah 30:17** – "For I will restore health unto thee, and I will heal thee..."

• **Psalm 103:2–3** – "Bless the Lord... who healeth all thy diseases."

Every appointment, every scan, every biopsy — I carried these with me.

Hope and Assurance

• **Romans 8:28** – "All things work together for good to them that love God..."

• **Psalm 34:4** – "I sought the Lord, and he heard me, and delivered me from all my fears."

• **Revelation 21:4** – "And God shall wipe away all tears... and there shall be no more death, neither sorrow..."

These verses helped me breathe again — they reminded me that no matter what the story looks like today, God has already written a beautiful ending.

 ᴀᴄᴋɴᴏᴡʟᴇᴅɢᴍᴇɴᴛꜱ

My heart is overflowing with gratitude as I reflect on the people God used to carry me through this journey. This book is not just my testimony — it is the collective strength, love, and prayers of so many who walked beside me, lifted me, and spoke life into me when I needed it most.

To my husband, Danny:

Thank you for holding my hand through every appointment, every tear, every fear, and every victory. Your quiet strength, your unwavering support, and your willingness to walk this valley with me made me feel safe, loved, and never alone. I love you more deeply because of all we've walked through.

To my children, Zachary and Madison:

You are the reason I fight with courage. Watching your faith rise and your hearts steady themselves in God gave me strength on days when my own strength felt thin. Madison, your sensitivity and compassion revealed God's tenderness. Zachary, your quiet strength reminded me of God's steady presence. I am so grateful to be your mom.

To my mother and father:

Even though you are no longer physically here, your love still covers me. Mom, you taught me how to walk with God. Dad, you taught me how to trust Him. Your faith is the foundation on which I stand. This book is as much your legacy as it is my story.

To my church family at West Houston Church of Christ:

Thank you for surrounding me with prayer, love, and spiritual covering throughout this journey. Your unwavering support — through worship, fellowship, encouragement, and heartfelt prayers — carried me in ways you may never fully realize.

You stood in the gap for me.

You lifted my name to God when I didn't always have the strength to pray for myself.

Your messages, your compassion, your embraces, and your steadfast faith were a source of comfort on some of my hardest days.

I am forever grateful for a church family that truly lives out the love of Christ — a community where faith is active, compassion is real, and prayer is powerful. Thank you for being my spiritual home, my refuge, and a reflection of God's heart throughout this entire journey.

To my sorority sister and my high school classmate:

After decades of silence, God brought you back into my life at the exact moment I needed prayer warriors. Your testimonies, your faith, and your obedience to reach out were divine assignments. You reminded me that God sends the right people at the right time — even 30 years later.

To the MD Anderson Cancer Center team:

Every single one of you was God-sent. From the schedulers to the nurses to the radiologists and surgeons — your care, compassion, diligence, and excellence saved my life. You looked deeper when others did not. You found what was hidden. You refused to stop searching. I thank God for assembling my medical team before the foundation of the world.

To my prayer circle — near and far:

Your prayers held me up when my knees felt weak. Your words carried me. Your love surrounded me. Some of you have no idea how your simple messages came exactly when I needed them most. Thank you for standing with me in faith.

Acknowledgments

To every reader:
Thank you for holding this book in your hands and walking through these pages with me. If you are in a valley, may my testimony be a whisper of hope. If you are weary, may these words give you rest. If you are afraid, may they give you courage.

Above all, **to my Lord and Savior, Jesus Christ:**
Every page, every breath, every miracle, and every victory belongs to You. Thank You for carrying me through the fire and bringing me out without the smell of smoke. May this book glorify You now and forever.

Closing Prayer

Lord, thank You for Your Word that comforts, strengthens, and sustains.

May these Scriptures draw every reader closer to You, fill their hearts with peace, and remind them that You are faithful in every season.

Let Your promises become their anchor, Your presence their comfort, and Your love their healing.

In Jesus' name, amen.

About The Author

Kimberly Allen is a wife, mother, and human resources executive whose life was forever changed when she heard the words, "You have Stage zero breast cancer." What began as private journal entries in her quiet moments with God became a powerful testimony of healing, restoration, and unshakeable faith.

Through scripture, reflection, and the gentle leading of the Holy Spirit, Kimberly discovered that fear never has the final word—faith does. Her journey is now encouraging women everywhere to lean into God's presence, trust His timing, and walk boldly in who He created them to be.

Kimberly lives in Houston, Texas, with her husband, Danny, and is the mother of two children, Zachary and Madison. She continues to write, teach, and inspire others to embrace God's peace in every season.